Alive in the Spirit
How to Name, Share and Seek More Spiritual Encounters

Rev. David S. Luecke, Ph.D.

Kravitz and Sons LLC
204 E Arlington Blvd. Suite B
Greenville, NC 27858

© 2026 Rev. David S. Luecke, Ph.D. All rights reserved.
No part of this book may be reproduced, stored in a retrieval system, or transmitted by any means without the written permission of the author.

Published by Kravitz and Sons LLC.
ISBN: 979-8-89639-646-8 (sc)
ISBN: 979-8-89639-647-5 (e)

Library of Congress Control Number: 2026903274

Because of the dynamic nature of the Internet, any web addresses or links contained in this book may have changed since publication and may no longer be valid. The views expressed in this work are solely those of the author and do not necessarily reflect the views of the publisher, and the publisher hereby disclaims any responsibility for them.

OUTLINE

Introduction
  Alive in the Spirit   7
    Name, Share and Seek More Spiritual Encounters
    Alive in Christ or Alive in the Spirit?
    The Father Wants Us to Ask for the Spirit
    Motivated by the Spirit
    Reason Plus Feelings
    Psychology of Religious Experience
    Give Spiritual Fellowship Priority over Church Organization

Part I **The Holy Spirit**
  Chapter 1 **How Do People Experience God in Their Lives**   23
    The Heart Language of God's People
    Recognizing the Spirit's Work in Your Life
    Recognizing the Spirit's Work in Others
    Less Obvious Religious Experiences
    Whispers of the Spirit
    Reliable Signs of the Holy Spirit
    How Do You Get More of the Spirit?

Part II **How the Bible Explains the Spirit at Work**
  Chapter 2 **Seek the Gifts and Fruit of the Spirit**   40
    Four Basics from Paul About the Spirit at Work in a Congregation
    The Holy Spirit Brings Special Energy for Ministry
    Gifts and Fruit of the Spirit as the Core of Paul's Understanding
    Word-Oriented and Spirit-Oriented Christians
    Learning from Spirit-Oriented Christians

Chapter 3 **The Spirit Brings Growth Beyond Conformity**   50

   The Limits of Village-Church Style of Ministry Today
   Life-Long Growth in Christ-Likeness Was Basic to Paul's Perspective
   Christ-Likeness and the Holy Spirit
   Gardener, Builder, Shepherd
   Different Pathways for Personal Journeys with the Spirit
   The Village Church and Very Large Churches Today

Part III How to Prepare For and Share Encounters with the Spirit

Chapter 4 **Cultivate the Soil of Personal and Church Life**   64

   Having More or Less of the Spirit at Any One Time
   Descriptions of the Journey
   Struggle
   Reaching Stage 4 Faith
   Recognizing a Transforming Experience
   Theological Repression
   Stories of Spirit and Memory
   Conversion or Awakening?

Chapter 5 **Share Stories of Personal Spiritual Journey**   77

   Having More or Less of the Spirit at Any One Time
   Descriptions of the Journey
   Struggle
   Reaching Stage 4 Faith
   Recognizing a Transforming Experience
   Theological Repression
   Stories of Spirit and Memory
   Conversion or Awakening?

Part IV How to Shape a More Spirit-Oriented Church Culture

Chapter 6 **Modify Your Church Culture to Thrive Spiritually**   96

   Decide to Thrive Spiritually
   The Holy Spirit and Church Organization

Face Leadership Fears
Loosening Up a Traditional Church Organization
Offer New Church Experiences the Spirit Can Use
Be Open to Supernatural Interventions
Develop a Spiritual Counter-Culture in Your Church
   1) Counter to "No More Miracles"
   2) Counter To "You Have To Do Special Things to Get God Moving"
   3) Counter To One-Dimensional University Culture
Post-Modern Opportunities

Chapter 7 **Change the Behavior To Change the Culture**   115
Recognizing a Church Culture
A Few Principles About Organizational Culture Change
Where to Start Changing a Church Culture
Influences on Behavior in Congregations
How Nehemiah Changed an Old Testament Culture of God's People

Chapter Discussion Guides   151
Key Passages on the Work of the Spirit Today   153

The wind blows wherever it pleases. You hear its sound, but you cannot tell where it comes from or where it is going. So it is with everyone shaped by the Spirit.
John 3: 8

Introduction to
Alive in the Spirit

Sailing close to the wind describes one of the most exciting experiences of sailing a boat. It puts the craft on the edge of being blown over and causes the need for counterbalance with sailors leaning out over the opposite edge. Keeping the sail set close to the wind offers speed and excitement. But it takes experience to lessen the risk. It also depends on teamwork.

The Holy Spirit is God's wind in our lives today. He can bring excitement to believers on their journey to becoming more like Christ. But we need experience and teamwork to reliably recognize the Spirit's leading. When in faith we do take risks to sail close the Spirit-wind, our personal and church lives will be far from boring.

Experiences of God are common in the lives of followers of Christ, according to Presbyterian pastor and clinical psychologist J. Harold Ellens. The reign of God is present where we are living by and with the spirit of God in our spirits. Our moments of the Spirit are those occasions when something develops in life that graphically or subtly illustrates that love works and grace heals. It is important to name those moments and tell others about them, so we become a people of the spirit, cultivating a culture of the Holy Spirit.[1]

Name, Share and Seek More Encounters

All Christians have encountered the Spirit. The Apostle Paul explains, "No one can say 'Jesus Christ is Lord' except by the Holy Spirit" (1 Corinthians 12:3). All who confess the Apostles' Creed declare their belief in the third person of the Trinity, the Holy Spirit.

Yet most Christians expect little of the Spirit today, especially those of us in traditional mainline church bodies, like Presbyterian, Lutheran or Methodist. We tend to leave the Spirit back in those days when Jesus and Paul said so much about him. We are too easily satisfied to keep Holy Spirit confined to the creeds. While we confess trinitarian beliefs about Father, Son and Holy Spirit, we practice binitarian ministry, emphasizing the Father and the Son, but for the most part forgetting the Spirit.

That is too bad. Our lives will be spiritually richer when we learn how to *recognize* encounters with the Spirit in our lives today, when we *share* these Spirit-encounters with others, and then when we deliberately *seek more* of the Spirit's influence for the days ahead.

We are used to thinking about objective truth—the kind we confess in creeds and catechisms. These doctrines about God the Father and the Son, about human sin and the Gospel are very important and set the context for the Father's and Son's advocate, the Holy Spirit, the third person of the Trinity. Always within the context of God's Word, the Spirit's job is to turn these objective truths into what is true for an individual believer. Such subjective truth amounts to the life-changing relationship of trust in the Christ who acted on our behalf. Such trust happens when the Holy Spirit comes to each personally as God's grace in action. "Having a personal relationship with Christ" is a good phrase to describe subjective truth.

Name an encounter when it happens. **Share** these encounters with others when and where appropriate. **Seek** more encounters by preparing yourself and inviting the Spirit. These pursuits will provide an improved rhythm for living the life overflowing that Jesus came to provide for his followers (John 10:10).

Such rhythm can amount to modifying a church culture, which is made up of a congregation's beliefs, values and behaviors passed on to others. Greater emphasis on the Spirit does not need to change *beliefs* about the Father and Son, but rather adds better understanding of what they do for us today through their Advocate. Let a church's *values* be modified to highlight *behaviors* that name and share recent encounters with the Holy Spirit and then the behaviors to seek more.

Alive in *Christ* Or Alive in the *Spirit*?

"Alive in *Christ*" is a bedrock conviction for followers of Christ. "Because of his great love for us, God made us alive with Christ" (Ephesians 2:2). Yet the title here is "Alive in the *Spirit*." A serious theological challenge lies behind this distinction. Traditional Christians confess that, his work on earth done, Jesus ascended into heaven and now sits at the right hand of God the Father Almighty. He is not with his followers here on earth at this time. Christ is present with us here now through his Spirit, whom he sends. God gives "life to your mortal bodies through his Spirit, who lives in you" (Romans 8: 11).

When Jesus comforted his disciples before his crucifixion, he promised, "I will not leave you as orphans' (John 14: 18). He assured them and us today that the world neither sees him nor knows the Spirit of truth. "But you know him, for he lives with and will be in you."

For the Apostle Paul Christ and the Spirit are interchangeable. We can find eleven pairings where in one passage he assigns a function to Christ and in another the same function to the Spirit. For instance, we have life through Christ in one passage; we have life through the Holy Spirit in a different passage. We are righteous in Christ; we are righteous in the Holy Spirit. Again, Christ is the alternative to the law; The Spirit is the alternative to the law.

Think of the relationship between Christ and Spirit as a two-sided coin. At my church we give out a grace and mercy coin. One side has a cross representing Christ and the words "Mercy is when God spared you what you do deserve." The other side has a dove representing the Holy Spirit and the words "Grace is when God gives you what you don't deserve." (hiscoin@gmail.com) By the mercy of Christ's gift of redemption we are saved eternally. By the grace of Spirit's life-changing fruit we can live better now.

Stories of personal conversion provide evidence of changed lives for born-again Evangelicals. Compare that to the promise-based message typically offered in traditional churches that do not feature how lives are being changed now in Christ by the power of the Spirit. The contrast gets sharper in comparison to Pentecostal churches that thrive on evidence of the Spirit as God's empowering presence. If individual lives are not being changed in traditional churches, the reason for their decline becomes apparent.

Leading New Testament scholar Gordon F. Fee did a detailed study of Paul's 169 references to the Holy Spirit that was formative for my fresh theological understanding. He writes, "It is this dynamic, evidential dimension of life in the Spirit that probably more than anything else separates believer in later church history from those in the Pauline churches. Whatever else, the Spirit was experienced in the Pauline churches; the Spirit was not merely a matter of creedal assent."[2]

The Father Wants Us to Ask For His Spirit

The invitation to ask for the Spirit is found in that very familiar passage of Jesus' teaching on prayer. "Ask and it will be given to you; seek and you will find; knock and the door will be opened to you. For everyone who asks receives; he who seeks finds; and to him who knocks, the door will be opened" (Luke 11: 9-10). It does not take long for Christians to figure out this promise does not extend to any and everything we might want. For that God reserves the right to say No or Later.

What Jesus is really talking about, however, comes two verses later. If fathers know how to give good gifts to their children, "how much more will your Father in heaven give the Holy Spirit to those who ask him!" Ask God to send his Spirit. He promises to do so.

God is quite capable of sending his Spirit without our asking and knocking. He does this when dispatching his Spirit to bring someone to faith and at times to initiate spiritual growth spurts. So why does God expect us to ask for the Spirit, whom he promises always to send? My answer is that he wants us to ask for specific movements of the Spirit among specific people. He wants us to form clear expectations so that we can observe when in fact the Spirit has moved. We are more likely to see what we expect than to notice something we are not looking for.

T. M. Luhrmann is Professor of Anthropology at Stanford University. She was a participant observer and researcher in two different Vineyard Christian Fellowships. She concluded that "coming to a committed belief in God was more like learning *to do* something than *to think* something. I would describe what I saw as a theory of attentional learning—the way you pay attention determines your experience of God."[3]

Just like anthropologists are trained to see what others miss, so Christians can be trained to see what many other Christians miss.

Luhrmann concluded, "So churches like the Vineyard teach congregants to find God in their minds and to discern which thoughts, images and sensations might be God's word. The congregants practice having minds that are not private but open to the experience of an external God. These faith practices change people." Luhrmann also observed that, "Whether those were authentic experiences of God cannot be determined by an "outside" observer. That is why being in a faith community is so important."

Motivated by the Spirit

Luke recounts that just before he ascended into heaven Jesus told his disciples that he was going to send what the Father promised, so "Stay in the city until you have been clothed with power from on high" (Luke 24:49). This is special power different from what is humanly available among us below. The focus of this book will be on understanding and getting ready for what Paul calls the gifts of the Spirit and a sub-category of fruit of the Spirit. These are the special power of the Spirit that get God's people energized in special ways.

Human motivation for ordinary people is something I know as a psychologist and former graduate professor of Organizational Behavior. The classic framework for understanding the personal needs people are driven to fill was offered by Abraham Maslow. It remains popular because it intuitively makes sense.

Primary are meeting bodily needs like hunger, followed by the drive to find predictable security. The needs for affiliation and status are at a higher levels. The highest, according to Maslow, is self-actualization.

Dominant needs shifted upward over the 20th century. Security was very important and motivating to workers in the early 20th century, and then affiliation and status needs took on more importance in the latter part of the century. Self-actualization seems more compelling to younger generations now.

Churches have been proficient at appealing to the range of human needs. Think medical missions in underdeveloped countries. Recognize the security offered by unchanging traditions and fortress-like church buildings in the inner city. In the first half of the 20th century there was a clear status ranking among Protestant churches. At the top were Episcopalians followed by Presbyterians. At the bottom were ethnic churches and Pentecostals. Many Christians were driven to change membership as they moved up socially.

The drive for affiliation with others became dominant in the 1950s and 60s with the out-migration from the cities to the suburbs. Most church bodies successfully planted many congregations when "joining" all sorts of social organizations was a strong drive. Such motivation is now disappearing, as documented by sociologist Robert Putnam in his report on *Bowling Alone*.[4] He observed that while bowling is now more popular than ever, the number of bowlers who join teams in organized leagues is plummeting. Such a diminished affiliation drive is affecting lodges, veteran organizations and also churches across the board.

The key question today is how churches should adapt. Surely the Holy Spirit was at work among Christians that developed church emphases addressed to human motivations dominant in these differing social and economic circumstances. Wherever Christians are gathered in the name of Christ, there is the Holy Spirit. But the cultural context for younger generations today is different from the context churches successfully addressed in earlier times of dominant needs for security, status and affiliation.

Christian churches will do well to adapt their own church culture now to address what motivation theory calls self-actualization—becoming uniquely you, growing into what you were meant to be. This emphasis fits well under Jesus' teaching that he has come so that his followers may have life in all its fullness (John 10:10). Paul looked at his leadership task as preparing God's people for works of service that build up the body of Christ until they become all they can be, reaching to the heights of the fullness of Christ (Ephesians 4: 11-13). He saw himself as a gardener planting seeds in individual lives that he expected to grow through the Spirit's work into self-actualizing, fruitful living.

Appealing to the more basic human needs did indeed enable the Spirit to energize Christian churches over the centuries. But human motivation alone has its limits, especially as our American culture becomes increasingly unchurched, because so many no longer see churches meeting needs they recognize. It is time to learn how to emphasize the supernatural motivation offered by the Holy Spirit.

Needing to focus on the practical, personal pay off from participating in a local church provides good reason to rediscover two aspects of Paul's ministry that were left on the periphery once Christian churches became well established centuries ago. One is his emphasis on the gifts and fruit of the Spirit. The other is his leadership self-image as a gardener and a builder rather than a shepherd. Spiritual gifts will be explored more in Chapter 2. More on ministry as gardening is in Chapter 3.

Reason Plus Feelings

The opposite of having feelings for something or someone

is apathy, literally being without passion. So many traditional churches today are victims of apathy. Members don't care the way the used to, which means that younger generations carry fewer positive associations with church life. To be apathetic about something is soon to see it as irrelevant to what is personally important. Evidence of their growing irrelevance is on display among withering traditional congregations.

In general, traditions emerge when they offer participants positive rewarding experiences, and traditions die out when current participants no longer find those experiences satisfying. The challenge is to find new ways to offer positive religious experiences in churches.

Diane Butler Bass was a popular speaker whose interpretation of larger movements helps explain to mainline churches their continuing decline. She observed that to put the words "experiential" and "belief" in the same sentence is asking for trouble in those circles. Noting how the modern Pentecostal movement first gave expression to the priority of experience, she reports the reaction of one pastor, "You mean we're all going to become Pentecostals? My congregation would rather die first! Faith isn't about feelings. It has to have intellectual content." Or as another said, "Why is it that the choice among churches always seems to be the choice between intelligence on ice and ignorance on fire?"[5] This dilemma, of course, is false. Between these extremes many congregations are working out a healthy middle ground.

What could be so wrong, anyway, with emotional experiences in church? Here is the issue: Do the emotions come first before you rationally figure them out? Such "raw" emotions are too often not of the Spirit and can become destructive. Or do feelings flow from perceptions subject to reason based on Scriptures? Such feelings can be the bedrock of church life. Psychologists call the first somatic, body-based theory and the second cognitive, brain-based theory.

New Testament scholar Matthew Elliott in his book *Faithful Feelings* observed that theologians over the centuries worked from a cognitive theory and therefore rejected emotions as irrational and unimportant. They picked up this understanding from Greek philosophy, like Stoicism, that focused on living at a level of reason higher than just emotions.

The whole endeavor of psychological counseling today works with cognitive theory based on the assumption that emotions can be changed by changing perceptions of their cause, and that such change is subject to reasoning. Elliott would label faithful feelings as Paul's fruit of the Spirit, such as love, joy, peace. In his study of emotions in the New Testament, he highlights how heart-felt convictions of the mind are accompanied by movement into action. Faithful feelings are an important part of the blessings God gives by way of the Holy Spirit.[6]

The role of emotions is highlighted today because so many Christians oriented to the Spirit first, called Pentecostals, concentrate on them. For churches oriented to the Word first these feelings need to be in the proper sequence: facts followed by faith followed by feelings. The *facts* are proclaimed in the Word. *Faith* is not only the noun for beliefs but is especially the verb for trusting those facts about God. God-pleasing *feelings* then flow from such faith. Spiritual leaders can be more confident in their ministry when they expect the Holy Spirit to work through this progression. Spirit-oriented churches would agree on the flow but are inclined especially to emphasize the third-stage feelings that can become very emotional. They often arrange their time together in ways that seemingly place primary emphasis on emotions.

Modern English does not lend itself well to naming

what now can be loosely described as feelings, emotions, or human spirit. That territory was defined several centuries ago as "affections" by American theologian Jonathan Edwards. For him affections are strong inclinations of the soul that are manifested in thinking, feeling and acting. Affections are different from emotions, which can be fleeting, superficial, and irrationally overpowering. For our times, think of "feelings" in the broad sense of being subject to reason and of motivating into action.[7] This will be important when we get to fruit of the Spirit in Chapter 2.

Psychology of Religious Experience

The academic psychology of religious experience has emerged to research and understand experiences loosely categorized as religious. The first academic to take the title "psychologist," William James gave the classic definition of a religious experience as "an incomparable feeling of happiness which is connected with the near presence of God's spirit," and "a sense of a presence, strong, and at the same time soothing, which hovers over me."

Of special interest will be studies of peak experiences like "conversion." Ralph W. Wood shows that experience of any sort must be described in order to be recognized. Language facilitates awareness and helps make it conscious.[8] Hence the need to "**Name It**" when one happens.

We should have a special vocabulary to recognize and talk about the Spirit at work around us. One phrase is "Spirit encounter." If you want to say spiritual experience, remember to capitalize the S so all know you are talking about an experience of the Holy Spirit. Other good phrases are "a God moment" or "a Holy Spirit sighting."

An "awakening" is a helpful word for those very special and rare times when one's Christian faith takes on significantly more meaning—when God became more real and personal in a new way, an a-ha experience when a light bulb goes on and life in Christ takes on a whole new dimension. It is comparable to Evangelical word "conversion," only awakenings can happen more than once in a lifetime. Awakenings will be developed in Chapters 5.

Addressing the classical conversion of someone who was not a Christian, H. Newton Malony concluded that human beings are so constructed that decisions made individually will not last and, second, the confirmation and support of others may be necessary for a conversion to be effective.[9] Hence the need to **"Share It"**—to describe to others our personal encounters with the Holy Spirit when they happen. Mutual conversation and consolation of the brethren is one of the basic means by which the Gospel offers counsel and help.

More recent psychological research on conversion recognizes there is a gradual conversion in addition to the classic sudden and even dramatic conversion. J. T. Richardson suggested that this second type is more rational than emotional; it flows from a compassionate rather than stern theology; and it emerges from a search for meaning and purpose.[10] Life-changing conversion to Christian faith does happen to some people at a specific time and place. But for most it is a process of growth in grace, with perhaps several memorable awakenings along the way.

Again, you will see more of the Spirit's movement if you have words to describe what happened, and you share this with others. J. Harold Ellens, the pastor and psychologist quoted earlier, described those moments as unique encounters when you can just feel something extraordinary happened that can only be attributed to the Spirit. Call them experiences of the Spirit, or special Spirit encounters. He explains,

The Holy Spirit is always a mystery, an intriguing agent

of God, full of intimations of God's nature, truth, and grace. These intimations speak spontaneously to our natures as we hunger for God. In this process, the Spirit is always evident, sometimes only in retrospect, always better than we thought it could be. One must have the eyes to see and the ears to hear, of course.

That is, these things are evident to those living life close to the wind, expecting the progress that comes from a vital spiritual quest. It is an intriguing and exciting thing, indeed, to live life always consciously anticipating how the Holy Spirit of God will show up around the next corner. The Spirit always does if we are expecting it.[11]

A major role of church culture is to offer language for identifying and explaining personal religious experiences. Christian hymns and songs have always served that function, as do the Psalms. More so than ever in the past, Christian church leaders need to accept the role of offering a special descriptive language for identifying and explaining personal religious experiences.

Encounters with the Spirit are more common than many think. I bring my own research through a survey of prayer life of over 500 randomly selected ordinary Lutherans. About half said they regularly experience a deep sense of *peace* and the strong *presence* of God during prayer. Striking was that about half agreed that "Prayer is the most satisfying experience of my life." These numbers were much higher than I and most of my pastor colleagues anticipated and gave direction to my thinking over the last thirty years.[12]

Yet traditional churches typically do little to encourage ordinary Christians to gain confidence and greater hope through sharing these personal experiences. We can change this.

Give Spiritual Fellowship Priority Over Church Organization

The congregations Paul led were truly spiritual fellowships, partnerships of believers drawn together by special motivation of the Holy Spirit. They made up whatever minimal level of formal organization they needed to solve problems they encountered, like how to make sure the Greek-speaking widows in their fellowship received as much support as the local Hebrew-speaking widows. For this they formally appointed seven Greek-speaking helpers, including Stephen (Acts 6).

Informal fellowships stand in contrast to the formal organizational structures that specialize in writing out various roles and relationships, as in a constitution. Extensive formal organization of churches rose to prominence especially in the recent half century with the explosive growth of management as a discipline for corporations and other enterprises.

It is no surprise, then, that churches, beginning in the 1950s and 60s, faced a major temptation to become a formalized organization like so many social clubs with their "members," "volunteers" and "committees." But the danger is that organizational methods will squeeze out awareness of Spirit-led ways of Christian fellowship. Because of the rise of the management mentality, organizational ways and the ways of the Spirit are in tension as never before in church history. The church leadership challenge in the 21st century is to find a middle ground that keeps the freshness of the Spirit-fed fellowship and the consistency of organizational structures that do not erect barriers to the Spirit.

Many churches were primed to apply new management techniques to their church leadership in the 1960s to 80s. I co-authored a book on *Pastoral Administration: Integrating Ministry and Management* that sold well. But judging by the results, that emphasis was not productive. Historic mainline pastors were the most interested. But the continued and accelerating decline of their churches forces the issue of what is wrong. In retrospect they hitched their future to a then-new leadership model with limited application to churches because it does not recognize the empowering wind of the Holy Spirit.

To assure Spirit-oriented leadership of church organizational structures will be more important in the future because of the new trend for just a few churches to become very large. Most of the growth in Protestantism is happening in those megachurches, as documented by the Hartford Institute for Religion Research.[13] Churches do not get big because they are well organized by human standards that reflect other current trends in society. They get big because the Spirit propels them and their organizational structure facilitates rather than hinders this foundational growth.

Where the Rest of This Book Goes

The next chapter presents further descriptions of religious experiences as **Part I**'s focus on recognizing encounters and experiences of the Spirit. **Part II** has two chapters that present the Biblical framework for what to expect of the Spirit and how he works. **Part III** shifts to the crucial subject of how to seek more encounters with the Spirit, both personally and as a congregation. **Part IV** addresses congregations that are moved to modify their present church culture to become more oriented to the work of the Holy Spirit in their midst.

Here is a summary of the positive behaviors to aim for in changing a church's culture. Pastors and congregations are encouraged to: Ask the Father to send the Spirit in specific ways. Tell stories of how the Spirit worked recently. Celebrate progress in personal spiritual journeys, especially in the form of major awakenings to a higher level of spiritual understanding.

Offer a greater variety of opportunities for encounters with the Spirit. Be willing to recognize God's supernatural interventions in healings. Make a conscious decision to cultivate soil for the Holy Spirit and to remove church-culture barriers that block him. Then the Holy Spirit can do more of his refreshing, renewing work among those gathered as the congregation.

The Holy Spirit shapes human spirit.
John 3: 6

CHAPTER 1

How Do People Experience God in Their Lives?

Is there a more basic question for Christians and their leaders to ask in this 21st century than, How do people experience God in their lives today? Ways of previous generations are not working as well now in younger generations. Word-oriented churches rightfully insist that the facts about God's ways are objectively true. The question is how they become subjectively true for individuals. When and how do believers attach trust and feelings to the Gospel? Faith without feelings remains superficial and probably boring.

Biblically, it is the Holy Spirit's work to bring hearers of the Word to such subjective experiences. This is the job description Jesus offered to Nicodemus, who approached him one night to seek better understanding of what this new rabbi was teaching.

Jesus explained he was all about the coming of the kingdom of God that you cannot see without being born again. Now Nicodemus was really curious and asked, "How can a man be born when he is old?" Jesus answered, "You must be born again of water and the Spirit. This Holy Spirit shapes human spirit."

Most English Bibles translate that key verb as "begets." The Spirit begets human spirit. The Greek dictionary of the New Testament offers a secondary translation of "to influence," like a teacher influences students. The Holy Spirit shapes human spirit.

Touching human spirits is the Holy Spirit's job. Spirit is a well-used word the meaning of which is hard to pin down. But we know a highly "spirited" person when we see one. The opposite is to be "discouraged", which describes a condition of the heart. Other words for a low spirit are depressed, anxious, unloved, or gloomy. Significant here is that their opposite is what Paul describes as the fruit of the Spirit, the major sub-category of gifts of the Spirit. These fruit include love, joy, trust, peace, patience. While these can be described as human qualities or characteristics, they are best regarded as feelings that express a heart condition. They are deeper than head knowledge.

"Spirit" in the original means wind. Jesus pointed out that you cannot see the wind but you can hear it. We might add that we can see the wind's effects in the movement of leaves and in the coolness a gentle breeze brings. How the natural wind blows is something we can identify with our senses of sight, hearing, and touch. The wind makes differences that are "sensible," or observable. Observable, too, are changes the Spirit wind can bring to the feelings of believers. This heart work is in addition to head work by which the Spirit enlightens believers with better knowledge of what the Word teaches.

Imagine yourself as Nicodemus. The practical question I am asking on your behalf is, How does the Holy Spirit work today in my life and my congregation? What observable differences should I look for? How can I prepare myself so the Spirit can do his special work better?

The Heart Language of God's People

The Bible presents many facts about God and how he relates to the humans he created. It teaches such basics as sinful human nature and the salvation won for us by Jesus on the cross, now offered by God's grace. We learn about the next world where the life of God's people will be even more abundant that it is now. We can learn from the Bible about the many promises God makes to his people. The details are worked out in doctrine books. These address head knowledge.

To find out how God's people feel about his actions and promises, we need to turn to language different from logical propositional truths. Feelings are expressed best in images and metaphors of poetry. The book of Psalms is the best source for this kind of inspired heart language. Psalm 23, The Lord is My Shepherd, is the best and most beloved psalm for putting words to feelings—the feelings engendered by the Holy Spirit. Here is an interpretation that stresses feelings.

With God as my shepherd I *feel full* of all I need. In him I find the *peace* of lying in a green pasture and walking along a quiet stream. My anxious soul is *refreshed* by him. He gives me the *confidence* to walk in paths of right behavior. He *takes away fear* when I face uncertainty and *comforts* me with his presence. I feel his *powerful love* when he provides for me in hard times and assures me I am special. He provides such abundance that *my cup overflows with blessings*. I *trust* he will always love and bless me with goodness. How great it is to feel the *presence* of the Lord now and forever.

Three key words can summarize what the Spirit brings to God's people: feelings of peace, presence and power. Do Christians always feel at peace with God and the world? Of course not. Our sinful nature causes us to feel anxious and unloved. Are Christians always confident that God is present comforting us throughout their daily lives? Of course not. Our human nature is to trust only ourselves. Do Christians always feel the power of God working things out on their behalf? Of course not. Satan wants us to depend only on our own meager powers.

But there are times when these positive feelings of peace, presence and power rise up in our consciousness. Such times can seem like breakthroughs when a new refreshing mood shoves aside an old sour mood. This is the Holy Spirit touching human spirit. You can notice the difference in yourself and also in others. We can learn to see shifts toward more love, joy, peace, trust, patience, kindness, gentleness, faithfulness, goodness and self-control. This is the fruit the Spirit works to grow in God's people.

Recognizing the Spirit's Work Your Life

The Apostle Paul had a dramatic experience of God and also a slow, over-the-years formation by the Holy Spirit. The dramatic one is his well know conversion on his journey to Damascus in Acts 9. We note that God sent Ananias to help him understand and share what happened. The slower formation we know little about. It started with the three years he spent in the desert after his conversion, a place Jesus, too, sought out before he started his ministry. According to Paul's report in Galatians, a total of fourteen years (Galatians 2:1) passed before he went to Jerusalem with Barnabas, who had sought him out in his home town of Tarsus and supervised a year of ministry internship (Acts 11: 25). It is reasonable to expect that Paul spent a lot of his unrecorded years explaining to others what happened to him and even preaching in the Galatian region near his home in Tarsus. Somewhere in those years Paul had worked out the centrality of grace in God's relationship with his people, as evidenced so powerfully at his conversion. He also came to much greater depth of understanding of how the Spirit works changes in the believer's heart, as the Spirit did in his own. Paul is by far the clearest and most applied interpreter of God's grace in action.

When he writes about what the Holy Spirit can do among God's people, you can confidently assume this is what the Spirit did to him over those years. He learned to look into the future based on his own past experiences of the Spirit. You, too, can do that.

- Have you found that your understanding of faith has moved beyond childhood knowledge to greater willingness to live with Jesus as Lord of all your life? That was the Holy Spirit at work (1 Corinthians 12: 3).

- Have you found that certain desires of your sinful flesh have lessened and even gone away? You experienced how, living with the Holy Spirit, you were less inclined to gratify desires of your old sinful nature (Galatians 5: 16).

- Have you experienced feelings of enslavement to pervasive fears that inhibit joyful living? The Spirit lessens them as he helps you cry "Daddy," confident of yourself as his child (Romans 8: 15). Is there movement in that direction that you have noticed in yourself lately?

- Have you noticed yourself more inclined to be involved in a congregation, perhaps teaching Sunday School or taking on administrative responsibilities? The Holy Spirit has been working on you, giving you extra motivation to do what you now find to be satisfying (1 Corinthians 12: 7).

- Have you found yourself experiencing a spiritual act of worship in decisions to sacrifice what seemed important in order to live a life more pleasing to God (Romans 12:1)? Recognize the Spirit at work.

- Have you experienced a special sense of unity with other

Christians, perhaps in a time of worship or when decisions were made? That was the Holy Spirit at work. Have you experienced such unity at a special conference with Christians? Thank the Spirit (Ephesians 4: 3-6).

- Have you found this week or last month a greater sense of love, joy, peace, patience, or gentleness? That was the Spirit working these fruit in your life. In years of teaching fruit of the Spirit, I found that the fruit wanted more than any other is patience, especially by those with children. Have you become more patient with your children lately? That's the Spirit. Do you want more patience? Ask the Father to send his Spirit.

- Have you found yourself frustrated speaking only words of human wisdom and seeking opportunities to express spiritual truths in spiritual words (1 Corinthians 2: 13)? This tug helped me recognize that, as well as I was doing, I was not at home at a secular university and to go teach at a Lutheran university. It also explains the satisfaction and joy I find in turning insights from psychology of religion into spiritual words.

Can you prove that any of these positive movements in your life came from the Holy Spirit? No more so than you can prove God exists to someone who does not want to see him. This insight happens when the eyes of your heart are enlightened (Ephesians 1: 18). It takes the Spirit to recognize what the Spirit has done in your life. This is what Jesus taught Nicodemus: You cannot enter the kingdom of God unless you are born of water and the Spirit. The Holy Spirit does shape human spirit (John 3: 6).

Recognizing the Spirit's Work in Others

- Wherever someone is encountering Christ's call to follow and is hearing the good news of grace in Christ, there is the Holy Spirit at work. Where a believer is participating in that encounter through personal witness and life, there is the Spirit in abundance.

- Wherever presentations of the Word bring greater insights and illumination to someone, there is the Holy Spirit at work, especially so when greater understanding is awakened in the heart (Ephesians 1:18).

- Wherever a believer's new life in Christ becomes stronger and more evident, there is the Holy Spirit at work. Look for him working this outcome especially through means of "the mutual conversation and consolation of brethren," in Martin Luther's phrase.[14]

- Wherever a person is considering whether or not to attend church on a Sunday morning and feels the tug to do so, there is the Holy Spirit at work, especially so when relationships with others in the fellowship help bring that affirmative response.

- Wherever two or three come together in the name of Christ, there he is in a special way through the Holy Spirit (Matthew 18:20). Look for the Spirit's work in improved relationships within a congregation and beyond it.

- Wherever there is special boldness, or wisdom, or determination among Christians, there is the Holy Spirit in special ways. Luke, the writer of the Gospel and Acts, describes followers with such characteristics as being "filled with the Holy Spirit." This description can be applied today to church members recognized as having special wisdom, courage or faith.

- The Spirit also brings freedom, and his work can be seen whenever a follower of Christ finds new levels of joy

- Wherever Christians come together with special energy and sing with gusto and intensity, there is the Holy Spirit (Colossians 3:16). "Spirit team" is a new name for cheerleaders at sporting events. When God's Spirit touches human spirits the joy can be like that of a high-energy event happening among those gathered in the name of Christ.

- Consider this viewpoint of Paul for spotting the Holy Spirit: The hallmark of the Spirit is freshness and renewal. God promises the Spirit will put a *new* heart and a *new* spirit into his people (Ezekiel 36: 26). Paul tells the Romans that the Spirit brings *new* ways different from living by rules (Romans 8: 1-4). He tells the Corinthians that *new* life-giving relationships come through the *new* covenant of the Spirit (2 Corinthians 3:6).

Some would understand the new life brought by the Spirit as a one-time event—at conversion. But Luther understood it as frequent, even daily process of drowning out the old nature in us through repentance and letting the new nature come forth and arise. Being made new again—renewal—is the Holy Spirit's work (Titus 3:5). The Spirit's way is movement, not status quo.

Paul explains to the Corinthians that the Holy Spirit transforms us into Christ-likeness with the movement of "ever increasing glory" (2 Corinthians 3:18). We are to be thus transformed by the renewing of our minds (Romans 12:2). The Spirit does that with individuals.

But he also can do so with congregations. The work of getting members aligned with Christ and with each other for ministries that build up the body of Christ should have the goal of reaching together to the very heights of the fullness of Christ (Ephesians 4:13). Whatever an individual Christian or a congregation might be reaching for now, there is more the Spirit wants to give and do. Settling for existing conditions is not the preferred outcome for life in the Spirit.

Less Obvious Religious Experiences

One of the greatest Roman Catholic theologians of our times, Karl Rahner, wrote *The Spirit in the Church* in 1977. It was his effort to put perspective on the charismatic movement that was strong especially among Catholics, Lutherans and Episcopalians in the 1960s and 70s. Those in the movement often had overwhelming experiences of the Holy Spirit in their personal lives, reflected in very joyful singing and dancing, intense prayer and usually speaking in tongues. Rahner responded, Yes, but remember the Spirit usually works in normal ways. In fact, often his presence is not obvious.

According to Rahner the Spirit of grace and freedom can work in a Christian even in these unglamorous ways:

- When a person does his or her duty where it can only be done with the terrible feeling that he or she is doing something ludicrous which no one will thank him for.

- When a person is really good to another person from whom no echo of understanding and thankfulness can be heard.

- Where a person obeys not because he or she must and would otherwise find it inconvenient to disobey, but purely on account of that inconceivable thing called the will of God.

- Where the leap into the darkness of death is accepted as the beginning of everlasting promise.

- Where one dares to pray into a silent darkness and knows that one is heard, although no answer seems to come back.[15]

In 2007 the media spread the news of an apparent crisis of faith in Mother Theresa. This information came from a book containing this letter she wrote to her spiritual confidant: "Jesus has a very special love for you. [But] as for me, the silence and the emptiness is so great, that I look and do not see,—listen and do not hear—the tongue moves [in prayer] but does not speak ... I want you to pray for me—that I let Him have [a] free hand." Her spiritual superiors considered this a spiritual strength—that she could persist in her calling even without feelings of affirmation from God. Such commitment could only come from the Spirit's movement in her life.[16]

We Protestants have a lot to learn from Christians in a church culture where duty, obedience and even grim determination can be spiritual acts. This may open up new appreciation for our church ancestors of previous generations who did not focus on emotions of joy and for whom love of others was sometimes hard to see.

Whispers of the Holy Spirit

We can envision God as a father and Jesus as a son. How do you envision a spirit? At Jesus' baptism Mark tells us that the Spirit came down on him like a dove. I have come to think of the Holy Spirit as a dove sitting on my shoulder and whispering into my ear. Christian living is a process of learning over time to listen to the Spirit's whispers.

The Spirit's role is explained by John as a *parakletos* in the original, which can be translated as comforter or counselor. A better translation is *advocate*. The Spirit is God's advocate in our lives. The Spirit communicates in whispers we can easily fail to hear.

In *The Power of a Whisper* Bill Hybels shares how he is very cautious and even defensive about "God told me" language. He tells how he hears God as a whisper and goes on to share many of his whisper experiences as well as whisper stories of others he knows.

Hybels writes that "From Genesis to Revelation, the constant refrain of Scriptures declares that our faith is relational—God listens when we speak through prayer, and we are to listen when he speaks through his whispers. In that earlier era, I longed for a sense of whispers like those, and thankfully, over time, I would learn to hear them."[17]

For me the clearest "God told me" experience came when considering a possible call to plant a church in my home town of Cleveland, Ohio. A lot of pieces of the puzzle of where to go next came together at about 4:00 pm on a Monday afternoon. That evening I announced to the family at supper that God told me where we were going next. Until then I had personally never used that phrase. Later with all the frustrations and disappointments of church planting, I drew comfort and energy from being convinced this is what God wanted me to do.

I recently experienced a loud whisper from the Holy Spirit in work I have been doing with our sister church body in Haiti. On a trip to a church site in a city damaged by the 2010 earthquake we were envisioning how much better the work of ministering to others and of building houses would go if we had a guesthouse for visiting teams. I can remember exactly where I was standing when I had this strong urge to put down a significant amount of money to buy property for this guesthouse. The whisper said to talk to a specific woman in our group. So I asked her if she could put down the same amount. It was a short exchange: If you do, I will. We did. With the help of LCMS World Relief and Human Care, there are now two guesthouses in different cities damaged by the earthquake. That initial investment proved crucial to starting the momentum that brought these results.

Go back to the image of the Holy Spirit, like a dove, sitting on your shoulder whispering and advocating what God wants in your life. To be a Biblical Christian, you also need to imagine someone else sitting on your other shoulder. Satan is God's adversary who wants to separate us from him. Peter gives us the image of a roaring lion seeking whom he may devour (1 Peter 5: 8). Pick your favorite image of the adversary but preferably something more realistic than a red devil with a pitch fork and tail. The internet world is used to designing symbolic avatars. I like to envision Satan as an ugly crabby guy who is always whining.

Is It Really the Holy Spirit I Am Hearing?

When you do hear a whisper that gets your attention, how can you determine if it is the Holy Spirit or the crabby whining foe?

In his discussion of *Hearing God,* Dallas Willard presented the three-lights test, originally named for finding a safe entrance into a difficult harbor in Italy. When all three are aligned in the same direction, you can grow in confidence that an intended action is God's will. The lights are:

1. The circumstances you find yourself in, by God's providence.

2. The impressions of the Spirit—what we are calling here the whispers of the Spirit.

3. Scriptural standards.

In the words of Frederick Meyer, "God's impressions *within* and his word *without* are always corroborated by his providence *around".* These are the three lights that combined give guidance for discerning God's voice. Willard discussed extensively how these are not a formula that can be simplistically applied, for each of those lights takes spiritual experience to recognize.[18]

I would add a fourth source of guidance in determining who is whispering into your ear. This is the counsel of well experienced Christians. Certainly for major decisions when you think the three lights are in alignment, wisdom lies in the request that other experienced Christians reflect on your assessments.

Where the Holy Spirit comes, there is enthusiasm. But it might be just the human energy and excitement that good cheerleaders can evoke. How do you know it is truly in-Spirited? Denial can easily carry the day among those who are not used to looking for the Spirit. The Apostle Paul would counsel that you really have to look for evidence of the Spirit through eyes of faith. But such eyes only come through the work of the Holy Spirit. Isn't this just a circular argument? In human terms, yes. But Paul would say, So be it. You are really addressing actions of God that are beyond simple human understanding and yet apparent to those enlightened by the Holy Spirit.

After years of discussion, the time came for the board of our church to make the decision about whether and how much to build and how much to borrow in what was the third major building project in ten years. There were good arguments for and against the proposal. Opinions were strong on both sides. The meeting had the potential to result in major conflict. But not so. Full consensus emerged with enthusiasm to go ahead. I could not help but recognize that the Holy Spirit, the dove of peace, was present. It helped that at the same time in a different room the director of prayer ministries had gathered a group that was praying for clear direction.

Reliable Signs of the Holy Spirit

In his first letter, John warns his friends, "Do not believe every spirit, but test the spirits to see whether they are from God" (4:1). What is the test? "This is how you can recognize the Spirit of God: Every spirit that acknowledges that Jesus Christ has come in the flesh is from God, but every spirit that does not acknowledge Jesus is not from God."

In addition to the three-light test, more practical guidance comes from Jonathan Edwards, powerful preacher and prominent Reformed theologian in what is now recognized as the first Great Awakening in eighteenth century New England.

A second and a third Great Awakening occurred in nineteenth century America. The Pentecostal movement of the twentieth century is considered by some to be a Fourth Great Awakening. The core controversial issue in all four revivals remained the same. One side emphasized religious emotions as the essence; feeling the love of God was most important. The other taught that the heart of true religion is right thinking; emotions are fickle and often lead astray.

Jonathan Edwards was decidedly Word-oriented. He argued against a shallow human-oriented view of spirituality. As noted in the introductory chapter, Edwards insisted that religious experience is centered in what he called the "affections"--strong inclinations of the soul that are manifested in thinking, feeling and acting. "Soul" meant the deepest and most essential part of the human person—what the Bible calls the "heart."

Affections can be either good or bad. The difference is that the good lead us toward God and the bad away from God. It is important to not be misled by bad or shallow affections, which Jonathan Edwards went at length to describe. While such affections can be a genuine manifestation of the Spirit, each can have other explanations, such as prideful, show off quoting of many Scripture passages, or self-serving eloquent talk and passionate praise for God, or pharisaical devotion to religious activities. This is not to say such activities are false. But they can have other motivations and in themselves are less than reliable indicators of the Spirit. They need to be accompanied by more reliable signs that reflect a closer relationship with Christ. Some examples are

- a lasting indwelling of the Holy Spirit that produces a new nature apparent through lives that show a difference,
- a new spiritual sense reflected in love of God that does not come from self-interest,
- a new kind of convicted knowing and genuine humility,
- a hunger for God and a Christ-like Spirit,
- Christian practice.[19]

How Do You Get More of the Spirit?

"Growing in grace and knowledge" is an intriguing phrase Paul's colleague the Apostle Peter used in giving a farewell wish to those reading his second letter. We recognize how to bring about growth in knowledge. On our own we can gain more knowledge of Scripture geography and history and master dictionary definitions of Biblical words.

But how do you grow in grace? Grace is not under our control the way we can gain knowledge on our own with time and determination. By definition, grace is a gift given freely. This is the meaning of the word we use to translate the Greek *charis* as gift by grace. God through the Spirit initiates gifts that allow us to grow in our capacity to become more Christ-like. This happens as we discover greater readiness to energetically serve others (gifts of the Spirit) and as we experience changes in our feelings of love and joy in all their forms (fruit of the Spirit).

The root for the word *charis* is *chara*, which means joy or gladness. *Chara* is the word used in Greece today to wish a blessing on someone else. It is a wish for someone's well-being. God's grace is meant for your well-being. If you want more of the blessing of joy and the other good fruit, put yourself where the Holy Spirit can work on you and give you the lasting fruit that comes only from above.

You can't get to the grace for Christian living and service on your own. It is not something someone can command you to do. Inspirational messages can bring a day or two of change. But lasting growth in love, peace, patience and other Godly fruit has to come as a gift of God through his Holy Spirit.

So, how do you get more of these gifts? In short, you ask for the Spirit to work on you and change your heart, and then you put yourself where the Spirit can get to you and do his heart-changing work step by step. You do that by staying tuned to God's Word and staying in the company of other Christians. This is how you grow in grace.

You will get even more of the Holy Spirit when you are ready to recognize he is indeed supernaturally present today. Was the special measure of the Spirit's work true only for Bible people in Bible times? I grew up learning that the miracles in the Bible were only true for that time, but once the Christian church was established, miracles no longer happen. Hence, don't expect any today. The same filters led me to see that being full of the Holy Spirit is something that happened only in Bible times. Hence you cannot expect special interventions of God today. Hence everything in church life today is under human control, with some symbolic reference to God the Holy Spirit.

Are you willing to join Paul in the belief that God's way

of interacting with people is true for all times in the Christian church? His way is by sending his Sprit to influence personal lives and the church partnerships these believers form. Thriving church life is not under our direct control. When we try to do church on our own, our routines tend to turn into something so humanly ordinary that few would recognize anything special of the Holy Spirit in it. Thriving in the Spirit comes at God's initiative. Our job is to prepare the soil of church life so the Holy Spirit can best do his advocacy and influence. More on this in Chapter 4.

Now about spiritual gifts, brothers,
I do not want you to be ignorant.
1 Corinthians 12:1

CHAPTER 2
Seek the Gifts and Fruit of the Spirit

Of all the cities where he ministered, the Apostle Paul stayed the longest in Ephesus. For the two and a half years there, he was in effect running a practical seminary for church planters "in the lecture hall of Tyrannus" (Acts 19: 9). Many of his "disciples" would already be leading congregations or would go on to plant new ones. Some certainly would have been linked to the other six congregations described in the book of Revelation, all of which were within a hundred miles of Ephesus.

Imagine daily discussions about solving church problems, like those they kept hearing about in the new church in Corinth that Paul started several years earlier. The questions they would be asking would certainly include these: What makes a Christian church different from all the other religious clubs so prevalent in Roman cities? God as father and son they could understand. How does the Holy Spirit fit in? What can we expect from the Spirit? Where should we look to see this Spirit at work?

Four Basics About the Spirit at Work in a Congregation

Paul's summary from these discussions appear in the twelfth chapter of his first letter to the Corinthians. He explains his purpose in the first verse, "Now about matters of the Spirit, brothers, I do not want you to be ignorant."

His first teaching is that "No one can say Jesus is Lord except by the Holy Spirit." Thus the Holy Spirit has already been at work moving any and all believers into saving faith. Such faith comes at God's initiative.

Second, he teaches to be aware of *charisma* given by the Holy Spirit. The gift given is *charis*. A gift *received* becomes *charisma*. The plural for gifts received is *charismata*. Paul begins his discussion of different charismata by using two other phrases to describe what they look like. They are different *ministries of service* and different *energies* for doing them.

Third, these expressions of the Spirit are for the common good of the congregation. They are not giftings to individual believers to be enjoyed privately perhaps as a sign of special status. They are given to the fellowship through individual participants acting in service to others.

Fourth, a different and additional key emphasis in Paul's teaching about gifts given by the Spirit comes at the end of chapter 12 in his transition to the beloved chapter 13 on love. He distinguishes a subset of spiritual gifts that he calls the greater gifts for the most excellent way of living together as a congregation. Chief is love, without which fulfilling life together is difficult. To the Galatians he describes these as fruit of the Spirit. These outgrowths of the Spirit's work are character traits and the feelings that accompany them. All have to do with building up healthy and productive relationships basic to church life.

Lost in the translation of *charisma* as gift is recognition that we have here Paul's second great teaching on *grace*, the English word usually used for *charis*, the gift given. The first he states most clearly in Ephesians, "For it is by grace you have been saved, through faith—not by works, so that no one can boast." We are saved at God's initiative. In 1 Corinthians 12 he explains that we receive motivations as gifts given by the Spirit at God's initiative. They are expressions of his grace. We do not earn them. But we can ask for them, recognize when they are given and better prepare ourselves for more such giftings.

The Holy Spirit Brings Special Energy for Ministry

Paul's major point in 1 Corinthians 12 is that in each congregation of believers the Spirit is already at work motivating all participants to contribute different acts of ministry for the common good. Such gifting might begin with natural talent, but it is not a gift to the congregation until it is put to use in that church. It is not the individual who determines his or her special gifting, but rather the congregation that discerns who does what well. This is motivation very different from reluctantly serving on a committee. When unique Spirit-giftedness of individuals becomes the basis for their service in the fellowship, they have a much higher sense of focused energy and Spirit-given satisfaction.

The leadership challenge is not only to identify special giftings but especially then to encourage and guide each participant to put his or her own gifting to work in the congregation, as we can see Paul doing in the twelfth chapter to the Romans. "If it (this gifting by the Spirit) is to serve, let him serve; if it is teaching, let him teach; if it is encouraging, let him encourage; if it is contributing to the needs of others, let him give generously; if it is leadership, let him govern diligently; if it is showing mercy, let him do it cheerfully."

So many traditional congregations today report in frustration, "We can't get anybody to do anything in church." This especially becomes a symptom of organizing like a social club with many committees that annually need to recruit volunteers to be fitted into pre-determined organizational boxes, whether or not they have spiritual motivation.

Paul's way is to start with individual believers who are specially motivated by the Spirit and guide them into productive ministry in the fellowship. The formal organization exists to shape and guide the spiritual fellowship. This primary fellowship is the church of Christ. The formal organization and governance structure are not the real church. They are human inventions that exist to serve their underlying spiritual partnership.

What are these *charismata*, giftings the Spirit distributes among individuals for the good of all in a congregation? They include unusual wisdom, knowledge, faith, along with special abilities to preach, teach, administer and heal. All cannot do everything equally well. There is nothing controversial about this observation. Giftings of this sort would be regarded as quite normal today.

Do you, the reader, have a special gifting from the Spirit for your involvement in a congregation? You can recognize such a gifting when you enjoy doing something in your church and you receive affirmation that you do this well. Do you look forward to helping or serving others? Do you like to personally encourage others in their faith? Perhaps you receive affirmation that when you lead a project, you do it well and find this satisfying. Do you enjoy being generous with your resources? Do you look forward to opportunities to teach children or adults? Do you find satisfaction in fixing things in the church building?

The listings Paul gives in 1 Corinthians 12 and Romans 12 are meant as examples. In your own words, what do you find satisfaction in doing at church? But recognize that the second part of identifying your spiritual gift is to get affirmation from others that they appreciate what you are doing. Some take pleasure in singing, but perhaps do not do this well. Without affirmation, be cautious about considering your talent as a special gifting of God for the congregation. Some want to lead but discover few want to follow.

The next chapter will discuss the overall leadership challenge of encouraging diverse expressions of Spiritual giftings in church life. Unity can become hard to maintain. Paul learned to seek and rely on the fruit of the Spirit working on individual hearts to make them more loving, patient and kind to each other. The opposite and easier way to reach and maintain unity is to hold expectations to the low minimum that all can do. But such a congregation will inevitably come up short on spiritual passions.

But Paul also affirmed the ability to speak in an unusual language. This gifting is not important enough to appear in his other listing of *charismata* in Romans 12. Word-oriented churches have special difficulty with the Spirit's gift of speaking in tongues for the basic reason that it overrides the highly valued rational process; it is fundamentally non-rational. Indeed, speaking in tongues is for many Pentecostals a heart-language that becomes an issue only when some regard it as superior to rational head-language, as Paul warns against.

So why not concentrate on the cultivating the other more normal workings of the Spirit? Surely for centuries congregations have recognized and appreciated those fellow participants through whom the Spirit works for the common good.

The Fruit of the Holy Spirit Bring Empowerment for Relationships

Paul's fourth basic teaching is about what fruit to expect from the Holy Spirit. He presents a listing in Galatians 5: love, joy, peace, patience, kindness, goodness, faithfulness, gentleness and self-control. He says "fruit" in the singular, the outgrowth of the Holy Spirit's work within individuals. As with examples of gifts, these fruit are not an exhaustive list. Other terms like these show up his other letters.

That these fruit are relationship-oriented is clarified in his benediction to the Corinthians where he chose "fellowship" as the key characteristic of the Holy Spirit: "May the grace of the Lord Jesus Christ, and the love of God, and the *fellowship* of the Holy Spirit be with you all" (2 Corinthians: 13: 14). The action most characteristic of the Holy Spirit's work is to bring us into greater fellowship with the Father and the Son and then to make changes in us to prepare us for constructive relationships with others around us.

In sum, if you want to see the Holy Spirit at work around you, look for human behaviors that reflect gifts and fruit of the Spirit.

Gifts and Fruit of the Spirit As the Core of Paul's Understanding

What makes this book different from so many others on the Holy Spirit is its fresh understanding of Paul's teaching on the gifts and fruit of the Spirit. Ever since the Christian church got institutionalized in the fourth century, these teachings on the gifts of the Spirit have been left on the periphery of what is important for church life together. In its organizational form the church made a sharp distinction between clergy and laity. The ordained clergy themselves were regarded as God's gift.

Little was expected of the rest, the laity, whose role it was to participate in the rites and to support the clergy.

A new perspective started emerging in the 1970s and 80s when Pentecostal Christians put their special interest in the gift of speaking in tongues into the context of the larger teaching of all the gifts of the Spirit in 1 Corinthians 12. Consultants developed spiritual gift inventories for improving church leadership by trying to identify those participants with one or the other of the range of gifts. The straight-forward action then is to encourage each to put their gifting by the Spirit into practice in the life of the congregation. This practical expectation is already a major shift away from the old understanding because of the assumption that leadership roles are open to all.

I have been teaching, applying and writing about the themes of 1 Corinthians 12 and Galatians 5 now for thirty-five years. The more I work with them, the more I see them moving from the periphery of Paul's thoughts to the very core of his theology and leadership approach. These gifts of the Spirit are his second great teaching on grace. First is salvation by grace through faith. Second is by grace living an abundant Christian life.

Word-Oriented and Spirit-Oriented Christians

The sixteenth-century Reformation yielded three major branches of Protestantism: Lutheran, Reformed (Calvinists) and Anglican (Episcopalian) whose descendants dominated Protestant Christianity up to and through the first half of the 20th century. My roots are Lutheran.

Those in this Reformation heritage remain strongly oriented to using reason to interpret Scriptures as the authority for Christian faith and life, often appearing to discourage any emotions. Meanwhile in the last half of the 20th century the Pentecostal movement came to prominence in America and world-wide. These Christians are strongly oriented to directly experiencing the Holy Spirit. Over the last one hundred years traditional Word-oriented Christians and leaders have often clashed with Pentecostal Spirit-oriented Christians over the roles of reason and emotions in church life. Re-discovery of Paul's full understanding of spiritual gifts opens the way to narrowing the gap.

Circumstances of the sixteenth-century Christian church led the Reformers to shy away from fully developing Biblical teachings on the third person of the Trinity. They feared the Spirit's work would get mixed in with the superstitions rife at that time. They also resisted radical interpretations of the freedom brought by the Spirit that could turn into social revolution, like the disastrous Peasant's Revolt in Germany in 1525. Luther wrote wonderful hymns to the Spirit before that year. Afterwards, the Spirit receded in in his thinking. Human social control was highly valued by John Calvin as he modeled theocracy in Geneva.

In effect, the Reformers set the dimmer dial of the light switch on low for the Third Person of the Trinity. It is time now to move the dial up to receive more of the light and energy the Holy Spirit can bring today. This book explores how churches of the Reformation can to do that while remaining faithful to their classical heritage. Besides Reformed and Lutheran, these mainline church bodies today include Presbyterian, Methodist and Episcopalian. Highly Word-oriented Baptists can work at dialing up their dimmer switch, too.

The traditional mainline churches are now often called old line. Once dominant in American society, they have all been on a 50-year decline in membership, now at an accelerating rate. Meanwhile Pentecostals are growing explosively world-wide. This is reason enough for classical Protestant churches to take another look at how to cultivate the work of the Holy Spirit in their midst.

All Christian churches recognize the third person of the Trinity, the Holy Spirit. In our classic traditions we pray for the Spirit's special work to enlighten believers and to bring heartfelt changes. But we do not identify what the changes look like, nor do we celebrate such growth when it does occur. Our priority is to turn the lights on bright for head knowledge. Yet historically we keep the dimmer switch dialed low for heart change. The challenge for low-expectation churches is to dial up the dimmer switch to expose more of the work of the Spirit in changing hearts.

Returning to the Earliest Church Charismatics

By any standard, the growth of Pentecostal expressions of Christianity has been phenomenal. A hundred years after its start in 1906, the movement worldwide was estimated to include 558,000,000 adherents. Some observers project it will reach one billion by now. Even secularists admit there seems to be an "S" factor at work in the continuing dramatic growth of this movement world-wide.[20]

In his study *Global Pentecostalism* sociologist Donald distinguishes five expressions of Pentecostalism. Several he calls "classical" in denominational expression. Most relevant here are the last two. To one he gives the title "Independent Neo-Pentecostal," often founded by religious entrepreneurs "who embrace the reality of the Holy Spirit and package it in ways that make sense to culturally attuned teens and young adults, as well as upwardly mobile people who did not grow up in the Pentecostal tradition." Miller considers them to be the cutting edge of the movement.[21]

The fifth type Miller distinguishes is "Proto-Charismatic Christians." They may be open to special manifestations of the Spirit but do not feature them. "They are simply attempting to follow the example of Jesus and the model of the early Christian church, which they see as being filled with manifestations of the

Spirit." I propose that traditional Protestants aim to become like proto-charismatic churches.

Learning from Spirit-oriented Christians

In what follows I will try to make the best case for how we Word-oriented believers can learn to thrive in the Spirit and then teach these ways to others. What I offer is solidly based on Scripture and, in my view, does not contradict anything in classical Reformation theology.

I offer the simple premise that more effective ministry by Word-oriented congregations will happen as we figure out how to recognize and purposefully cultivate the work of the Holy Spirit we confess to be already in a congregation's midst. My aim is to point ways toward becoming "early-church charismatic Christians" cultivating the normal work of the Holy Spirit.

For many established church bodies like Episcopalian, Lutheran and Catholic the word charismatic brings back bad memories of the "charismatic" movement of the 1960s and 70s that turned out to be very divisive in many congregations. But that was more than fifty years ago. It is time to take a fresh look at the other charismata Paul taught and relied on.

Churches in decline need to ask this question. Is theirs a God problem or a church culture problem? That there is dramatic Spirit-driven growth going on worldwide suggests God the Spirit is alive and still powerful. Church decline points to the conclusion that an inherited church culture is falling out of sync with our rapidly changing American culture.

The world is changing too fast around us to continue to overlook the power source that the Apostle Paul relied on for the growth of the Early Church. The Spirit continues to energize new churches in other parts of the world. It is time for more of us to seek that special energy from on high in traditional American churches.

*You are God's garden. I planted the seed, Apollos watered it,
but God made it grow.*
1 Corinthians 3: 6,9

Do not conform any longer to the pattern of the present time.
Romans 12: 2

CHAPTER 3
The Spirit Brings Growth Beyond Conformity

My brothers and I used to spend summers back on the Illinois farms of various uncles and aunts who lived in the same community. Those summers exposed us to a very different life style from what can be seen living in the suburbs today. I remember riding with a cousin on his morning run to pick up milk cans from farms. It seemed every other farm family was a relative to a second or third degree. Such social fabric gives a tremendous sense of identity and belonging.

But there are drawbacks. Big city people today do not know very well the dynamics of village life. Conformity is basic. Everyone knows and watches everyone. To be very different from others brings penalties. As the saying goes, the nail that sticks its head up gets hammered down. Tied to their farms, they all know they have to live together for the rest of their lives. It is safer to base unity on everybody doing the same thing than to take on the challenge of maintaining unity while recognizing different spiritual temperaments and different stages of spiritual growth among participants. Village church culture emphasizes passing the faith on in well-known traditional ways that become the basis of preserving unity.

These stable and confining relationships have major implications for how church is practiced in a village. The need for predictability tends to keep in the background the Holy Spirit who wants to shake up relationships and bring individual growth that increases diversity in a congregation. Villagers become wary and critical toward neighbors who upset the routines, especially those who report strong emotional experiences of God.

The conformity of village life shaped the cultures of churches that still carry their European roots. For centuries after the Reformation about eighty five percent of the population lived in rural settings. Such a high percentage of rural population held through to the end of the nineteenth century even in America.

Village roots are apparent in church heritages that still talk about a congregation as a parish. This is a geographic term, and everybody living in the village boundaries was treated as a congregation, whether or not they take on formal membership. Traditional parish talk has little to do with a primary spiritual fellowship. Loyalty to the village church and its denomination can be assumed, and motivation by guilt can be effective.

The old ways, however, do not fit well the new reality. Now American population is down to at most about ten percent rural, meaning that about ninety per cent live in urbanized areas. This huge demographic shift alone should call into question the value of village-shaped traditions.

In contrast to such conformity, the Apostle Paul recognized that the hallmark of the Holy Spirit at work is freshness and change. Unfortunately significant change is usually not welcomed in most traditional churches. Paul told the Romans, "Just as Christ was raised from the dead through the glory of the Father, we too may live a *new* life (6:4). Paul also expected the Spirit to bring ongoing discoveries of newness and freedom into the life of Christ's followers. To the Corinthians he points out, "The Lord is the Spirit, and where the Spirit of the Lord is, there is freedom" (II; 3:17)—the freedom to break out of old ways and to try new ways of living and relating to God

Many congregations and pastors wind up doing the same old things with the same people in the same old ways and thereby close the door on what new things the Spirit might want to do among them. The Spirit's inclination is to change people, not leave them in a rut.

Trying to Carry on Village Style of Ministry Today

We can recognize at least two practices today that were shaped by village-church ministry. One is confirmation of 14-year-old children baptized as infants. The other is emphasis on the separation between clergy and laity.

Village churches baptize infants with the assumption the family will remain in the congregation and also with the congregation's intent to nurture their children into the faith that was professed for them by others. Confirmation became a graduation ritual by which the young adult personally affirms this faith. Such personal affirmation of baptismal faith happens typically at the end of the eighth grade, because until well into the twentieth century that was the end of formal school education. Teaching the church body's catechism was basic. Catechisms apply God's Word as knowledge and are aimed at heads, with the assumption hearts will follow.

There are sound theological reasons for baptizing infants based on recognition that by grace God takes the initiative in his relationship to individuals. The real issue is 14-year-old confirmation. It made sense in the sheltered environment of a village where all shared the same values and encountered few challenges to their faith.

Something more is needed, however, when children now go to schools that do not recognize the role of God in creation and where many students have lifestyles with very different values. Many church-raised children do not survive the transition with their entry-level faith intact. The head knowledge from confirmation needs to be strengthened with experiences that bring heart conviction. Fourteen-year olds at least ought to be taught to expect challenge and to hear from previous young adults who have worked through their doubts into deeper faith.

Going back to the years when the pastor was the only literate and educated person in the village, that old church culture made a clear distinction between clergy and laity, a distinction not found in Scriptures. The pastor personally does most of the ministry, joined in larger churches by others who are ordained or commissioned. The lay member's role is to support this ministry by making financial contributions and regularly attending church. For many this is done with a sense of duty and habit. There is little room for recognizing spiritual gifts among laity.

Those stable village traditions worked well during population growth and migrations from the farm to the city in the early parts of the twentieth century in America. They persisted through the big-city migrations out to the suburbs in the 1950s and 60s, when there was a strong desire to join something and to replicate the churches they came from. But now in the 21st century it is time to recognize that what worked for traditional churches in earlier decades is not working well anymore in urbanized areas, as evidenced in the continued decline of congregations that still practice village traditions.

To put the issue differently, today the Holy Spirit does not seem to accomplish as much as he used to in the soil of congregations and ministries shaped by village culture. Such soil needs to be cultivated more creatively.

A little story told to me by a friend illustrates the two cultures. She was talking to a sister who is a member of a city remnant-church with only twenty or so members in attendance. My friend relayed excitement over her congregation's project of serving free coffee and hot chocolate in the middle of the night to the people lined up to enter stores early for the Black Friday sales after Thanksgiving. The sister responded, "You're just trying to be different from us." Such a put down is a classic example of village church thinking persisting into the 21st century. Conformity is assumed. Without change, not many years of life remain for the sister's once-thriving congregation in the city.

Life-long Growth in Christ-likeness Was Basic to Paul's Perspective

Village church culture tends to assume that confirmed adults are mature Christians. If any more growth is expected, this would be in knowledge of the Bible, out of which should come greater faith and guidance for living. The village has little vocabulary to describe changes in heart condition brought by the Spirit and then the changed perceptions that follow. Emphasis is much more on comfort than on challenge.

Paul's understanding of maturity is quite different. No one ever reaches it. He tells the Ephesians that their local body of Christ should continue to be built up until all become mature, reaching to the height of Christ's full stature (Ephesians 4:13). The Greek word translated as "mature" really means becoming all that you can be. In today's terms, it means self-actualization. Because the standard is Christ-likeness, we will never reach full maturity as a Christian in this life.

He told the Corinthians, "We are being transformed into his likeness with ever-increasing glory, which comes from the Lord, who is the Spirit" (2 Corinthians 3: 17, 18). In other words, the Spirit repeatedly changes us to become more like Christ and thereby to reflect more of God's glory. In all my years of Lutheran grade and high schools, Lutheran colleges, Lutheran seminary and in listening to thousands of sermons, I don't remember any special reference ever being made to this passage. It does not fit the prevailing mindset, which expects little from the Spirit and does not anticipate the big changes of personal transformation.

Note how Paul assumes ongoing growth in personality-changing fruit of the Spirit:

- We thank God because your faith is *growing more and more*, and the love every one of you has for each other is *increasing* (2 Thessalonians 1:3).

- May the Lord make your love *increase and overflow* for each other and for everyone else, just as ours does for you (1 Thessalonians 3: 12).

- All over the world this Gospel is *bearing fruit and growing*, just as it has been doing among you since the day you heard it and understood God's grace in all its truth (Colossians 1:6).

- Now he who supplies seed to the sower and bread for food will also supply and i*ncrease* your store of seed and will *enlarge* the harvest of your righteousness (2 Corinthians 9: 10).

The Apostle Peter, Paul's close colleague, shared the same assumption about continued growth in fruit of the Spirit. He writes, "For if you have these qualities in *increasing measure*, they will keep you from being ineffective and productive in your knowledge of our Lord Jesus Christ" (2 Pet 1: 8). The qualities Peter specifies right before that passage are these: faith, goodness, knowledge, self-control, perseverance, godliness, brotherly kindness, and love. These same qualities are what Paul expected as the fruit of the Holy Spirit's influence.

In that passage Peter adds the intriguing conviction that it is possible for Christians to be ineffective and unproductive. Literally, he says barren and unfruitful. Clearly he expected growth in the fruit worked by the Holy Spirit, beyond whatever we can produce on our own. Christian faith brings eternal salvation, but it should also produce continued life-changing growth in this world.

The Holy Spirit Generates Christ-likeness

What does Christ do in our lives today and how does the Holy Spirit figure in? The second and the third persons of the Trinity are easily confused with each other, and it is much easier to develop a relationship with a son than with a blurry spirit.

The Apostle John gives us the job description for each. The Spirit's job is to serve as God the Father's and the Son's advocate for what they want and offer in our lives. The Greek for this role is *parakletos*. Comforter is a weak translation. Councilor is better. Best is to think of an advocate, a lawyer or agent who offers what someone else is ready to provide. The Holy Spirit advocates for the Father and the Son and makes accessible what they offer.

John in his first letter offers a parallel job description for the Son, Jesus Christ. Using the same word *parakletos*, he writes that "If anybody does sin, we have an advocate to the Father in our defense—Jesus Christ, the Righteous One." Thus Jesus is our advocate like a lawyer in God's courtroom, and the Holy Spirit is the Father's and Son's advocate to us in our daily lives.

Here is how Jesus described the Spirit's job: "I will ask the Father, and he will give you another advocate to be with you forever—the Spirit of truth. The world cannot accept him, because it neither sees him nor knows him. But you know him, for he lives with you and will be in you. I will not leave you as orphans"(John 14:15). Later Jesus said "When the Spirit of truth comes, he will guide you into all truth; he will tell you what is yet to come. He will not speak on his own; he will speak only what he hears. He will bring glory to me by taking from what is mine and making it known to you" (John 16: 13).

The images of wind and fire were used for the Holy Spirit that first Pentecost. But for me those images do not seem very personal. I find it is easier to think of the Spirit's advocacy in the form of that dove that came down from the sky to sit on Jesus' shoulder at his baptism. This image can replace the oblong blur so many believers imagine the Holy Spirit to be. I have learned to picture him sitting on my shoulder throughout the day, whispering into my ear thoughts that would make me react in more Christ-like ways to what is going on around me. The dove urges me to respond constructively and warns against hurtful ways. The same Spirit gives the ability to discern the differences.

For Paul life-long growth in Christ-likeness is the best description of what Christian living is all about. We have four Gospels' worth of narratives about what Jesus was like, the values he held, the behaviors he showed, the claims he made. Various descriptions of growing more Christ-like process will be discussed in Chapter 5.

In Paul's thinking, when we are talking about life in Christ we are at the same time talking about life in the Spirit. They are two ways of describing the same experience, two sides of the same coin. To become more Christ like is to be filled more by the Holy Spirit.

Spiritual formation is a process of reaching higher and higher to the full stature of Christ (Ephesians 4:13). Do you want to become more like Christ? You can't do it on your own. Concentrate rather on receiving more from the Holy Spirit. With our own abilities and powers we cannot change and move very far toward Christ-likeness. But using those abilities and powers, we can cultivate the Holy Spirit's work in our hearts, and congregations can become better hosts of the Spirit.

Gardener, Builder, Shepherd

Paul told the Corinthians they were God's garden as well as God's building (1 Corinthians 3: 9). For him the work of ministry is cultivating the land that presents itself in the people of a specific congregation, promoting life-long growth in Christ-likeness. Given his emphasis on different gifts of the Spirit, I think he envisioned a garden of many different plants, not a field with all the same crop. He also focused on a second image of joining and building church participants together as a temple in the Lord.

Paul's gardener and builder self images got lost over the centuries in favor of the shepherd image, which Paul himself does not use.

Consider: "You are God's garden." "I planted the seed, Apollos watered it, but God made it grow." (1 Corinthians 3: 9,6). After Paul calls the Corinthian congregation God's garden, he goes right on to say "You are God's building. By the grace God has given me, I laid a foundation as an expert builder, and someone else is building on it." He expands the building image with this explanation to the Ephesians: "In Christ the whole building is joined together and rises to become a holy temple in the Lord. You are being built together to become a dwelling in which God lives by his Spirit (2: 21-22).

When Paul laid a foundation for a congregation, he was not only teaching them the life-changing truths of what God offers in Jesus, the Christ, through his Holy Spirit. He was also modeling how the Spirit works differently in individuals. He modeled how the leadership challenge is to build up and integrate growth-stimulating relationships among those who responded to the new Gospel of grace he proclaimed. Get the foundation of grace-oriented, Spirit-inspired relationships right, and a lasting and fruitful local body of Christ is easier to build up into a unique temple.

Your Perspective Compared to Paul's

Imagine you are a leader looking at 200 worshipers gathered on Sunday morning. What do you see?

Using the gardener metaphor, do you recognize their similarities and view those people as a field with rows of, say, corn or soybeans? Or do you focus on their differences and see a garden with many kinds of plants at various stages in their growth? Some are still children. Are the grownups all about the same? To be sure, your job as leader is much easier if you see mostly the similarities and expect little beyond their participation and support. Are they mostly the same from year to year or are you seeing change and growth in their character and relationships? Can you recall their individual stories of spiritual growth and journey which you have helped celebrate? Do you see spiritually healthy plants, or do too many show signs of failure to thrive.

Shift to the temple image. Are you seeing those gathered together on a Sunday morning as a one-room temple, or can you recognize a more complicated structure of many rooms under one roof? Are you focused mostly on maintaining this spiritual temple, doing the routine ministry tasks they expect? Or do you want to build it up into something different and better, even without growth in numbers? Is your ministry mostly encouraging and patching up what is there already? Or do you have in mind what *could be* there with a few renovation efforts or by taking on several remodeling projects, or by adding on a few rooms for those with special interests and needs? We are not talking about constructing physical rooms, but rather about building up the most Christ-like fellowship of those who are gathered in all their diversity.

An inherent problem in congregational ministry is getting beyond the limitations of one size fits all. It is the same message that all hear, and usually the same worship format as well as the same Bible classes. But the participants are not all the same size and don't give the same responses. Some are still beginners and others think there is nothing more to learn. A few learn by reading, more by listening, even more by discussion while many others learn by doing. Some sense God's presence best in traditional rituals and symbols, others in acts of service, still others by involvement in their community, and some by growing in knowledge. Pastors themselves tend to focus on knowledge and often are surprised by how few others share such a passion for the Word. Indeed while some few are passionate about their faith, many others are at best lukewarm.

Different Pathways for Personal Journeys with the Spirit

The constant temptation in life with other Christians is to expect others to experience the work of the Holy Spirit the same way you do. This is especially true for those in church bodies that emphasize their favorite gifting by the Spirit to speak in tongues or give prophetic utterances. Paul would point out that it is up to God to determine which gift of the Holy Spirit he will give to whomever he chooses. It is crucial to avoid implying that those with different experiences are somehow second-class Christians.

The differences start all the way back with basic temperaments people show from early age. It is one thing to know this in theory but something else to show the practical implications. Description and measurement became possible with the publication of the Myers-Briggs Type Indicator, which is now administered to two million people a year, mostly in corporate settings. The Myers-Briggs focuses on normal populations and emphasizes the value of naturally occurring differences.

One of the earliest applications of this indicator to prayer came with survey insights described by Charles Keating in *Who We Are Is How We Pray*.[22] That title would work as a heading for this section.

The Meyers-Briggs asks questions that assess on which end on four different variables you find yourself, and it yields sixteen combinations. The problem I found is that sixteen possible combinations are more than I can keep in mind and be able to move to practical application for participants. But the theory opens up a new understand of why it is important to offer a variety of opportunities for experiencing God in ways suited to more than one temperament.

Gary Thomas offers a much better application in *Sacred Pathways: Discover Your Soul's Path to God*.[23] He narrows the options to nine that intuitively make sense and can be found in Scriptures. These are:

The **Naturalist**: Loving God Out-of-Doors. Finds a walk through the woods to be very conducive to prayer.

The **Sensate**: Loving God with the Senses. Wants to be lost in awe, beauty and splendor of God.

The **Traditionalist**: Loving God through Ritual and Symbol. Likes structured worship with symbols and sacraments.

The **Ascetic**: Loving God in Solitude and Simplicity. Wants to be left alone in prayer.

The **Activist**: Loving God through Confrontation. Serves a

God of justice, and church fills a need to re-charge batteries.

The **Caregiver**: Loving God by Loving Other. Serves God by serving others.

The **Enthusiast**: Loving God with Mystery and Celebration. Wants to be inspired by joyful celebration.

The **Contemplative**: Loving God through Contemplation. Likes images of loving Father and Bridegroom.

The **Intellectual**: Loving God with the Mind. Drawn to explore basic issues in theology and church life.

This is not the place to go into a detailed exploration of these sacred pathways. That book is set up for you to do so on your own, with appropriate illustrations, identification of the characteristic temptations that come with each temperament, and a rating scale of six questions for each so you can identify which temperament seems most like you.

It should be no surprise that my temperament is the intellectual. I have many colleagues strongly oriented to ritual and sacraments. While I agree with the theology, I have grown more willing to admit that the sacraments have less resonance with me than it obviously has with them. Part of remaining an effective church and church body is to learn how to accommodate these different temperaments.

The Village Church and Very Large Churches Today

If a wide range of offerings is important for congregations in the future, then the future is increasingly with very large congregations.

One legacy of the village is a one-pastor, small congregation with perhaps 100 in attendance. Originally in a village, the size of the parish boundaries would provide a limited number of families within walking distance.

There is good research evidence that the future of Protestantism is toward megachurches with attendance of 1,000 or over. They continue to grow while average congregations are in decline. Also, they have a larger proportion of younger generations.[24]

How does a congregation become a megachurch? My conclusion is that it happens under an unusual set of conditions, many of which are beyond the congregation's control. They key factor seems to be movement of the Holy Spirit. When the Spirit is blowing, the congregation then has to run to add buildings, parking and staff to keep up with the growth. Like most things with the Spirit, his influence is easy to stop. In this case it would be by not accommodating more people.

The congregation I served has an attendance of about 1,000. We grew by 15-20% a year in the late 90s. We have been plateaued since. An essential part of the growth about twenty years ago was a feature article in the local newspaper about the new wave of contemporary worship, featuring our church with a large photograph on the Sunday front page. Our attendance went up by 200 in the following six months. No one can plan such media coverage. Somewhere in all that the Holy Spirit was at work.

This chapter and the previous have addressed the biblical framework for recognizing the Spirit at work. Central is Paul's focus on spiritual gifts and the subset of fruit of the Spirit. He had the leadership self-confidence to recognize the Spirit-given diversity among those gathered in his congregations. He was willing as well to rely on the Spirit to produce growth in fruit basic to living with differences. Both the diversity and life-long growth were lost in the village-church setting of congregations over the centuries. Rediscovering Paul's framework for ministry can bring new effectiveness and excitement to congregational life.

Others, like seed sown on good soil, hear the word, accept it and produce a crop.
Mark 4: 20

CHAPTER 4
Cultivate the Soil of Personal and Church Life

When my brothers and I spent summers on the Illinois farms of relatives, we saw that their major task in midsummer was to cultivate the soil between the rows of corn out in the field. The actual cultivator was a toe-like triangle that was lowered to about three inches below the surface and pushed along by the tractor, which would be outfitted for about six rows. It was a summer version of the deeper plowing in the springtime to plant the seed. Summer cultivating worked the soil to dig up the weeds and let rainwater penetrate more readily to the roots of the corn stalk. Working the soil yielded a better harvest.

Use this image of cultivating the soil to picture primary tasks of ministry. The seed to be planted and grow is God's Word. The harvest to look for is the gifts received from the Spirit in the forms of energy to do ministry and also in the fruit of love and better relationships, as developed in Chapter 3. From this primary harvest come greater passions to worship in spirit as well as truth, to absorb God's Word and to reach out to others with the Gospel and in service. The point here is that harvest will be greater when the soil is periodically broken up, that is, cultivated.

Working the soil is implied in the first parable Jesus told, the Parable of the Sower and the Seed (Luke 8). He used it to show how his ministry was all about initiating the kingdom of God in this world. Luther explains that the kingdom of God comes to us when the Father gives us His Holy Spirit, so that by his grace we believe his word and live a godly life. The parable of the sower identifies four kinds of soil. The seeds will not bear much fruit when they land on a hard path, or rocky soil or among weeds. The seeds that landed on good soil yielded a crop a hundred times greater than what was planted.

The challenge is to improve the hard, rocky and weedy soil as much as possible. Purposely cultivating the soil is important both in the lives of individual Christians and in their life together as a congregation.

Personal Preparation for the Spirit

Christian tradition rightly recognizes that the basic preparation for any encounter with God is repentance. Each needs to review and establish his or her relationship right up front. Basically this means acknowledging "I am sorry" for how I messed up. I confess the ways I have been less Christ-like than I should and want to be.

The Bible offers at least three images for how to approach God in repentance. One is the parable of the Pharisee and the Publican (Luke 18). This religious superman reviewed all the ways he was a good man, as if that will win him special favor with God. The publican looked down, beat his breast and confessed, God, have mercy on me, a sinner. The punch line is that those who humble themselves will be looked upon favorably by God.

A second similar image is in James' letter when he states God's view succinctly: "God opposes the proud but gives grace to the humble" (4: 6). This crisp proverb sets the context for the other Gospel in a nutshell about how God in his grace sent his Son that whoever believes in him will have eternal life (John 3: 16). The basic preparation for encountering God is to humble one self. Another way to state this is that when you are full of yourself, like the Pharisee, there is little room for the Holy Spirit to maneuver in your heart and soul. You first have to reduce the amount of yourself.

The third image is given by Isaiah when he sees the majesty of the Lord seated on his throne as the seraphs sang "Holy, holy, holy," their voices shook the temple doorposts and the temple was filled with smoke. The only thing a human can say in the presence of such majesty is, "Woe is me! I am ruined! For I am a man of unclean lips" (Isaiah 6: 5). Would that we could keep this image of God's majesty before us all the time. But over time we humans tend to cut God down to our size and let the Pharisee in us slip into our thinking.

In Chapter 1 I made reference to Jonathan Edward's description of reliable characteristics of an encounter with the Spirit. He also offered a description of his own feelings at his personal second awakening: "I had great sense of humility, brokenness of heart and poverty of my soul. My heart panted after this, to lie low before God, and in the dust, that I might be nothing and that God might be all; that I might become as a little child."[25]

In his special encounter with the Spirit, Edwards wanted to "become as a little child." The mystery of God kingdom is such that not only will it include children but indeed, as Jesus explained, it requires being like a child (Luke 18:17). Spiritual birth is as radically passive as physical birth; the chief actor is God through his Holy Spirit. Our preparation is to humble ourselves and to seek his mercy. This is true repentance

Personal Hard Paths, Rocks and Weeds

What are the hard paths, the rocks and the weeds in our personal spiritual lives? The *hard paths* could be the superficial routines we insist on following that keep us focused on other things, like sport, job, success, money, and even family. The seeds of the kingdom of God cannot even take root because there is no room in our busyness.

The *rocks* could well be our routines that make us feel religious without being drawn closer to God. God's kingdom occasionally breaks through with short roots. But the roots cannot go deep because we like our comfortable life and resist change.

The *weeds* could well be familiar distractions that we let choke out continued growth in our personal kingdom within. Weeds would be whatever keeps us from regular intake of God's Word through which the Holy Spirit works on our self-perceptions. Weeds could be whatever we let keep us from regular interaction with other Christians who can help us discern God's will in the circumstances we face.

Soil-Related Ministries in Congregational Life

Eugene Peterson, translator of *The Message* version of the Bible, offers a vivid description of a congregation as top soil for pastoral leadership.

Congregation is the topsoil in pastoral work. This is the material substance in which all the Spirit's work takes place—these people, assembled in worship, dispersed in blessing. They are so ordinary, so unobtrusively there; it is easy to take them for granted.

But this is the field of pastoral work, just as it is, teeming with energy, nutrients, mixing death and life. I cannot manufacture it, but I can protect it. I can nourish it. I can refrain from polluting or violating it. But mostly, like the farmer with his topsoil, I must respect and honor and reverence it, be in awe before the vast mysteries contained in its unassuming ordinariness.[26]

Envision the hard soil in a church as reliance on routines and traditions that offer little opportunity to make things new, which is the Spirit's specialty. The rocks might be hearts hardened by past conflicts and rigid dogmatism, in need for the Spirit to soften them. The weeds might be activities in a congregation that distract from the church's spiritual mission of helping God's kingdom come among those gathered through the Spirit's work.

My reaction to the three kinds of soil that yield low harvest is shaped by the pragmatic instinct of a church leader. Let's fix it. Let's improve the soil. While we cannot manage the Holy Spirit, we can work on changing the soil present in a congregation's life together. We can break up surfaces hardened by unchanging routines. We can add loose soil between the rocks. We can pull weeds out of our church life. Call these three steps part of skillfully cultivating the soil of church life.

Breaking up Hard Surfaces

Any congregation that meets regularly over the years develops routines and traditions for how they worship, learn, serve and work together. Over time the surfaces of these structures become hardened and closed to new expectations of what the Spirit can do in their midst. The soil will better host the Spirit's work when those routine expectations are frequently unsettled by new and different ways of sharing the Gospel within a congregation. Then more water of the Word can seep deeper into the soil of this church's life together. Then the Spirit can work more effectively on the roots of God's special kingdom wanting to grow in the heart of individual believers. When the routines and traditions of a congregation become hardened to new expectations, then that church is living mostly on memory without fresh energy. Over time the old spiritual energy runs out.

Increasingly, new definitions of the key words "spiritual" and "religious" are emerging to describe what is happening in declining denominations. According to historian Robert Fuller, "The word *spiritual* gradually came to be associated with the private realm of thought and experience, while the word *religious* came to be connected with the public realm of membership in religious institutions, participation in formal ritual and adherence to official denominational doctrines. . . 'Spirituality' is taken as a positive term, whereas 'religious' is often negative."[27]

For many observers, "religion" has become the villain in spiritual life. Note these titles of recent books: *Christianity without Religion*, *God without Religion*, and *Jesus without Religion*.[28] In the present context religion is what happens when church routines and traditions have become hardened surfaces with little new spiritual energy. Having spent my whole career serving institutions, I cannot join that bandwagon of casting off external forms. But as an insider I will observe that the routines and structures of many traditional churches are no longer in sync with our changing times. Traditional Christian "religion" needs to change its ways in order to become more "spiritual" for newer generations.

Dealing With Rocks

In Jesus' parable of the sower, the second place where seed landed is on rocky ground where there was little soil. "The seeds soon sprouted, because the soil wasn't deep. But when the sun came up, it burned the young plants; and because the roots had not grown deep enough, the plants soon dried up" (Mark 4: 3-8).

Practically speaking, there are only two ways to deal with rocky ground if you want something to grow there. Get rid of the rocks, or add soil.

But first define rocky ground in a congregation. I take this to be participants who remain very superficial in their interactions with God. They get enthused for a while by interaction with others in worshiping God or serving others, but soon settle back into old ways of avoiding the Word and staying distant from the Spirit. The roots of God's kingdom in their hearts cannot go very deep. Either pressures of life will dry up those roots, and these people fade away from the Spirit's reach. Or their hardened hearts resist the Spirit's continued work through the Word, and further growth of God's plant in them is stunted. Their church life becomes comforting routines and traditions of their religious rather than spiritual life.

"Throw these rocks out," is one response. The church is only for true believers, defined by various criteria. Pentecostals reserve church membership only for those who have experienced the second baptism of the Spirit by speaking in tongues. Or the congregation is only for those who have experienced a "true" conversion, as expected in many Evangelical churches.

But there is wisdom in the parable Jesus told right after explaining the seed and soils. While it is directed to weedy soil, it applies to rocky soil as well. When weeds appeared, servants asked the owner whether they should pull them out. The answer was no, because they might pull out some of the wheat along with them. Sort it out later. So, too, leave the rocks where they are. At least while they are present in a church, the Holy Spirit has additional opportunities to work on softening their hearts.

The Apostle Paul explained that just the confession of Jesus as Lord is work done by the Spirit. That is sufficient for eternal salvation. His theology was all about the Spiritual growth that comes afterwards. Much to the disappointment of many Evangelicals, traditional churches of the Reformation believe that just a head knowledge confession that Jesus is the Christ is sufficient for salvation and for participation in a Christian congregation. The pastoral leadership challenge is to foster ongoing growth of God's inward reign through the work of the Holy Spirit.

We need to recognize that such growth in discipleship was not much in mind for the Reformers who, focused on eternity, wanted to get the doctrine right and assumed that hearts will follow heads.

Add More Soil

So don't throw out the rocks. Add soil for deeper roots.

Adding more soil can amount to increasing the number of stories about how the Spirit impacts lives today, especially among existing members. More stories come by carefully cultivating the congregational "Holy Spirit culture" that Harold Ellens envisioned in the Introduction. He commented on the excitement of living life always consciously anticipating how the Holy Spirit of God will show up around the next corner.

One story Ellens tells concerned a friend of his waiting in the checkout line at a grocery store. "The lady ahead of her was struggling with her glasses, checkbook, pen, and paraphernalia. As she struggled, she remarked to the clerk that she was upset and confused because her mother was dying. My friend spontaneously expressed concern about how hard that can be. This led to an extended conversation in which she was able to share the burden of that stranger and communicate to her the consolations that my friend experienced in sailing her life close to the wind of the spirit, so to speak. This struck a responsive chord in the stranger's soul, and the upshot of the event was a great sense of strength and renewal for both persons."

Ellens stresses the importance of naming those moments as events "of the spirit" and then of sharing them with others so that they become a conscious culture of the Holy Spirit and are not forgotten. He proposes that developing such a culture means doing the following:

- Expect to experience the presence of God's spirit in tangible ways regularly.

- Notice those manifestations of God's spirit in ordinary and extraordinary moments and events.

- Name those moments as "of the spirit."

- Explain those moments to each other and thus raise the consciousness level of all.

- Continually recall together that those moments have happened and continue to happen.

- Come to think of ourselves as the body of Christ constantly made lively by that spirit of God, living in the expectation of more experiences of the spirit's presence to us in tangible ways.[29]

Pulling Weeds from Church Life

Let God decide whether an individual participant is a weed. The weeds to pull out of the soil of church life are those that creep into the structures leaders develop to shape and protect the interactions of their primary Spiritual fellowship.

Weeds are anything that distracts from the primary nature and mission of the fellowship gathered together as believers. Examples could be fund raisers, renting out facilities, even having meetings without invoking God's presence, and maybe even having special "fellowship" events. Our goal at the church I serve is to "make and grow disciples." In practical terms, this means don't waste leadership or congregational time or energy on anything not directly related to making and growing disciples. The rest is weeds.

In the Introduction I presented the challenge to give fellowship of the Spirit priority over church organization. Organizing gets formalized with such techniques as constitutions, carefully crafted goals, written job descriptions and assignments, designated work relationships. Such management practices have become a key part of our current American culture. This is a good news/bad news development for churches. The good news comes with skillful pastoral leadership that keeps the formal structure focused on the primary fellowship.

The bad news is when organizational techniques squeeze out recognition and reliance on the Spirit's often spontaneous influence on the hearts and motivations of the believer. Then such a congregation begins to look and act like any other social organization. Then it begins to resemble the many community clubs that are in rapid decline in America society today, offering opportunities for "involvement" without special motivation by the Spirit. Such congregations are likely to find themselves withering away to their final end sooner or later. While some may prolong life by renting out their facilities for income, this approach is likely to choke out the Spirit's influence even more.

Developing Spirit-led Community

James W. Jones, then professor of religion at Rutgers University, reflected on spontaneous fellowships that emerged in the American youth counter-culture movement of the 1960s. Communes of 20-somethings dropping out to live together "to realize one's potential, to get themselves together." He participated in some and shared his observations as a Christian.

Most of the participants he saw were searchers in "a circle of empty vessel, each waiting to be filled. Since every vessel is empty, no one has anything to pour into the gaping containers." Most of those communes got into trouble and fell apart in a few months or a year. He notes that in America only religious communes have survived any length of time. They have something to share with others.

Jones observed, "We on our own cannot create community no matter how hard we try. Community flows from a shared experience, an experience that fills individual vessels so they have something to pour out into the other vessels. This experience is the work of the Holy Spirit."

Many who could not live communally in small settings felt guilty about their failure. Jones counseled, "They shouldn't have; koinonia is a gift of the Spirit, not a natural human possibility. The experience of koinonia is something given us, not something we create. Christian community is not built by building Christian community. It is the side result of doing something else, like following the lead of the Spirit.[30]

The original Christian church of Acts 2 was a commune. "Selling their possessions and goods, they gave to any one as he had need." But very quickly that spontaneous fellowship had to get structured and administered. It started with appointment of Stephen and six others to oversee food distribution. Some thirty years later Paul had to increase the formal organization by giving to Timothy written job descriptions for leaders and also welfare-like rules about which widows qualify for support. Even at the very beginning there was no lasting alternative to developing structure and institutionalizing some relationships.

To use the now popular distinction between "spiritual" and "religion", pure spiritual fellowship will not last long without taking on some external forms now derided as just "religion." The challenge for the leaders of these external structures is to keep their focus on the primary spiritual fellowship that gives life to whatever forms are developed.

As our American culture gets increasingly used to administered relationships, a church's organization needs more pastoral supervision so the focus stays on the ways of the Holy Spirit. In management terms, the senior pastor is the Chief Spiritual Officer (CSO) and often will need to add the role of Chief Executive Officer (CEO).

A Call to Church Repentance

Part of cultivating the soil of church life is to hear Peter's call to those hearers gathered on the first Pentecost to: "*Repent* and be baptized."

An annual day of congregational repentance was part of the soil of good church culture left behind years ago in my church body. It was not just individual repentance but repentance by the whole congregation.

What that could be is shown in excerpts from the sermon by Pastor C. F. W. Walther in 1870, thirty-two years after the beginning of Trinity Lutheran in St. Louis. They had much to be thankful for—they had grown from a few to many, from a poor church to a wealthy one with a large sanctuary and school. Yet, "We are no longer what we were. Today should be a call to repentance." Whether they have truly gone forward or backward "hinges on how things stand, first, in respect to faith in God and, second, in respect to love to the neighbor. For just as only faith and love make a Christian into a genuine Christian, so these two parts alone make a congregation into a genuine congregation."

To this pastor, this congregation had gone backwards. With

respect to faith in God, "Instead of an eager digging for the gold of the truth in Holy Scriptures and in other good books, isn't there now among most of our members a running and rushing after earthy riches, after big business deals.

With respect to neighborly love, whereas they were once like a family, now "do not many all too often manifest indifference, yes, coldness over against those they know are brothers and members of the congregation? Is it not only too evident that, on the part of many, a respectable child of the world is regarded more worthily and highly than a brother or sister? Has not the zeal to win souls practically died out among us? Has not brotherly admonition almost entirely vanished? Does not 'backbiting and evil speaking' against brothers and sisters rule in almost all our meetings?

"Oh, let us therefor today above all appear before the holy God as a fallen congregation in genuine contrition and repentance. . . Oh, if today we return to God repentant and believing, this day will be the day of the rebirth of our congregation and a time of new visitation of God's grace and new, greater blessings will dawn up her."[31]

Since we live by the Spirit, let us keep in step with the Spirit
Galatians 5:25

CHAPTER 5
Share Stories of Personal Spiritual Journey

The first name given to Christians was People on the Way, on a journey. The Greek word shows up in English when we talk about the dashboard *odo*-meter in an automobile. This measures the miles that have been driven. It is really a record of journeys taken with that car.

A few years ago I had a Honda that took me on about 100,000 miles of journey. These are a blur, since they are mostly to and from the church office, on errands around Cleveland and visiting children. The odometer on my 1981 Pontiac station wagon, however, told a very different story. It took the family on two cross country moves and six summers of family vacation all around the West, including six scenic national parks. The most special of the Pontiac's journey were family experiences while the children were in grade and high school—camping in the Northwest, dodging forest fires in Yellowstone, seeing a bull fight in Mexico, mom reading to the children in the car for hours, kids squabbling who gets the "way back" in the station wagon.

We like to retell stories of those journeys, like spending a whole night sleeping in the station wagon because I did not stop early enough to find a motel room available. It rained most of the night so we could not open the windows much. Biffy, our dog, was this story's star, or villain, because he passed a lot of gas that night.

To tell one's spiritual journey is simply to recall personal memories from years of living in Christ. Where did it start—as a child or an adult? Some Christians have in focus their conversion experience at a specific time and place. Others always knew they were Christians from childhood on. More important than where the journey started is where a believer is right now. What were some of the high points and then also the low points? Sometimes the low points are necessary to get to the "mountain top" experiences.

"Spiritual journey" is a wonderful concept in the conversations of many Christians today. Personal stories of life with the Spirit are somewhat foreign to traditional church cultures, which tend to have a more static outlook on the Christian life, as if little of personal spiritual significance happens through their adult lives.

When Paul first saw People on the Way (Acts 9: 3), he recognized they were going someplace and not just to heaven. They were dangerous because theirs was a journey different from Jewish tradition. Years later he described them as on the way to becoming more mature people, "reaching together to the very height of Christ's full stature" (Ephesians 4:13). He urged them to go their way "in step with the Spirit." Over time an adult Christian should become a different person than when she or he first knowingly affirmed their faith.

Paul would say that if you are talking about spiritual journeys and you are not looking for the Holy Spirit, then recognize that you are not talking about Christian spirituality.

Having More or Less of the Spirit At Any One Time

Luke uses the unique and helpful phrase "full of the Holy Spirit," which he then couples with a specific characteristic to describe what that fullness brought. In Luke's Gospel Elizabeth was full of the Holy Spirit and *rejoiced* about her blessedness. Zechariah was full of the Spirit and *prophesized*. In Acts the apostles chose the seven helpers whom they recognized as full of the Holy Spirit and *wisdom*. In one passage Stephen was full of the Holy Spirit and *faith*. Peter and John were full of the Holy Spirit and proclaimed *boldly*. Barnabas was full of the Holy Spirit and *faith*.

These people of God had the Spirit with them always but occasionally more so at a specific time and place. Then they had the Spirit to a fuller degree that gave them unusual wisdom, faith, power or boldness. They certainly also would have had times when they had less of the Spirit at work in them.

The description of being full of the Holy Spirit at a certain time offers the image of each believer as a vessel or pot into which God pours his Spirit. Indeed Paul explicitly used that image when explaining to the Corinthians, "We have this treasure (the Gospel) in jars of clay" (2: 4:7). To Titus he used the vivid image of the Spirit being poured out upon us (2:6).

This image gets even better when we picture the vessel as having a hole in it. This hole in our personal pot is the sinful nature that remains with even the best of Christians. Resistance to the Spirit by our remaining old nature amounts to a hole out of which the Spirit leaks, sometimes to the point that the vessel is almost empty.

Even better is to add to this image the picture of the jar overflowing with what is poured into it. One of Paul's favorite words is usually translated as overflowing or excelling or abundant. Thus he tells the Romans about God's overflowing provision of grace (5:5). He encourages the troubled Corinthians to excel (rise even more) in Spiritual gifts that build up the church (I: 14:12). In nine other places he couples the word with one or the other fruit of the Spirit, such as overflowing love (three times), overflowing joy (two times), overflowing thanksgiving, and also overflowing wisdom and understanding. These forms of overflowing add depth to the Psalmists praise that "My cup overflows." This word for overflowing is the one Jesus used when explained how he came "that they might have the abundant life, life overflowing" (John 10:10).

What was Paul's major objective for the believers he was leading? He wanted primarily that they be filled by the Holy Spirit to the point of having so much of the Spirit that his gifts and fruit overflow in their lives of abundance.

Descriptions of the Journey

The all-time favorite spiritual journey story is *Pilgrims' Progress*, written in 1678 by John Bunyan and translated into 200 languages. The pilgrims are Christian and his wife Christiana. Each has a separate journey on the way to the Celestial City. Many characters try to lure them off the right path. Others help them on the way. The tempters include Formalist, Hypocrisy, Timorous, Mistrust, Ignorance, Giant Despair. The helpers have names like Good Will, Prudence, Faithful, Hopeful, Old Honest. On the way they have to pass through places like the Slough of Despond and the Valley of the Shadow of Death.

Recall Paul's examples of fruit of the Holy Spirit, like love, joy, peace, hope, faithfulness, self-control. Pilgrim's helpers represent those characteristics. We in turn are invited to take those roles in helping others on their way. The tempters are their opposite. John Bunyon knew well that a believer's spiritual journey is shaped by the ups of growing in the fruit granted through the Holy Spirit and by the downs of being distracted from them.

One helpful description of the journey is offered by Willow Creek researchers in their report *Reveal*. They divide the journey into four stages: 1) Exploring Christianity, 2) Growing in Christ, 3) Close to Christ, and 4) Christ-Centered. These four stages in turn yield what they call three movements for a believer's spiritual journey. The first is from Exploring Christianity to Growing in Christ. The second is from Growing in Christ to Close to Christ. The third is from Close to Christ to Christ-Centered. The questionnaire results give characteristic behaviors and attitudes that accompany each movement.[32]

These researchers wisely refrained from picking any one movement to call "conversion." In truth, a much better word is to describe each movement as an "awakening." Something happened that drew them closer to Christ. For every participant these awakenings will be unique to their personal journey. It would be fascinating to hear each journey story. The variety of circumstances and influences would make abundantly clear that in church life there is no "one size fits all." An interesting follow up to that research would be to interview respondents to hear their stories of what happened to them in those movements of the Spirit.

One of my favorite descriptions of the journey is by Janet Hagberg and Robert Guelich in their book *The Critical Journey: Stages in the Life of Faith*. For them stage 1 is recognition of God. Stage 2 is learning the life of discipleship. Stage 3 is the productive life, where most church professionals are included. Stage 4 is the very important journey inward. Getting to this point almost always involves "hitting the Wall," or an obstacle they cannot overcome with their ordinary efforts and skills. They try everything to scale it, circumvent it, burrow under it, over it, or simply ignore it, but the Wall remains. The authors explain that "The Wall represents our will meeting God's will face to face and our discovering anew whether we are willing to surrender."[33]

The Wall could be a failed marriage, or lengthy unemployment or very serious illness. The key is to learn to give up dependence on self and to surrender to God's loving providence. Then the Spirit's refreshing fruit of love, joy, peace and hope can come to greater expression.

The biggest awakening of my personal spiritual journey came in February, 1992 when I was recovering from an acute viral infection. Serious illness is a good time for the Holy Spirit to do his work. I was home brooding about what was, among other things, the apparent failure of our biggest church plant outreach. The previous October we made our major effort according to a program called The Phone's for You. We had called every phone number in the target three suburbs to invite them to a special worship service. The big event was in November. But by February there was no visible impact on attendance. Now what? In my brooding I was a failure and probably would have to find ministry somewhere else. This was embarrassing for someone with high visibility in Church Growth circles. Public failure is a great time for the Spirit to do his work.

I had hit the Wall. I was doing my part. Why wasn't God doing his part? Over several weeks the Spirit worked on my heart until I came to a peace-giving acceptance. So be it, even if I have to sell the house. Having built several, I found the prospect of letting go of this new house to be the hardest part. After surrender came new energy and resolve. A year later we found and remodeled a building in a park-like setting that became our church home. It made part of the foundation I left behind.

Struggle

Meditation, prayer and struggle—*meditatio, oratio, tentatio* in Latin—was Martin Luther's prescription for the training of ministers. It is a good formula for the spiritual growth of any Christian. The third ingredient, struggle, is key to turning head knowledge into heart-felt conviction. Christian faith often stays superficial until it gets tested by some circumstance in which a believer's life does not go as expected and his or her self-concept of life with God is shaken.

The *tentatio* of spiritual life can result in a heart-felt experience that brings new intellectual insights. But many do not recover. They walk away from their superficial faith and look for some other approach to finding meaning. They are more likely to rebound in faith when they have stronger Christians around them who can interpret what is happening. Doing so is a fundamental purpose for the fellowship of Christians that is basic to church.

Struggle cannot be taught. It happens one by one through personal response to unique circumstances. But we can observe what it is like in others and learn how God worked it out their lives. It is the personal struggle of a "before" condition that sets up the compelling "after" story of a movement to greater convictional faith. Such stories are worth telling and hearing. This is more likely to happen when the story fits into a category and has a special vocabulary to describe what happened. Then this transition to deeper faith can be celebrated with others. The story can give hope to others that the Spirit may help them, too, grow.

A pastor colleague of mine told a sad story that happened in his internship year when he accompanied the pastor on a hospital visit. The woman talked about how she was so angry with God about her condition. The pastor said, "No, you are not" and proceeded to tell her why she should never be angry with God. What a squandered opportunity for spiritual growth. Such thinking is pure village culture where the need to keep up appearances of faithfulness stifles struggle and therefore misses opportunities for growth.

Reaching Stage 4 Faith

A young staff member commented about "When I became a Christian in college." This intrigued me because I knew she had been baptized as an infant, gone to Sunday School, was confirmed and was much involved in youth activities in her church. I challenged how she could say "When I became a Christian in college." She acknowledged that, yes, she knew she was a Christian before then, but her faith took on new meaning through involvement with a campus ministry. Those in that ministry had taught her the phrase.

To my way of reckoning, she had experienced an awakening. More specifically, she had moved from Stage 3 of faith development to Stage 4. Either way, God was at work in her life, and this high point in her spiritual journey was cause for celebration. May she have more awakenings in the years to come.

These stages of faith come from highly regarded developmental psychologist James Fowler. He posits that faith, rather than belief or religion, is the most fundamental category in the human quest for relation to transcendence. Fowler was a professor of theology and a Methodist minister.[34] His language is very academic. I prefer descriptions of the stages offered by theologian Thomas Droege and will use his titles for the first four of Fowler's six-stage framework to Christian faith development. Consider these stages:

Stage 1 "God's just like my mommy and daddy." —the literalism characteristic of the pre-schooler.

Stage 2 "What's fair is fair!" —characteristic of a child seeing God as a stern law giver.

The Stage 2 remains the level of many adults whose approach to life is that you get from God what you earn. This leaves the uncertainty about the final judgment and whether your good deeds outweigh your sins. I have encountered many Christians who had known about God's grace all their lives but never quite caught the significance of his love and forgiveness for daily living. Knowledge alone does not always convert into a heart on which the Spirit has had much impact. Culture usually trumps preaching, and the routines of a village church culture can leave personal faith unexamined in stage 2.

Stage 3 "I believe what the church believes." —characteristic of a teen's interpretation of faith and story as taught by authority figures.

Stage 3 is typically at child confirmation level. It is a faith taught by authority figures. At this stage, believers tend to have a hard time seeing outside their box and don't recognize that they are "inside" a belief system. It is unrealistic to expect a mature faith from fourteen-year olds.

Stage 4 "As I see it, God is . . . —characteristic of young adults who form their own opinions on the way life is to be lived and how God acts in the world.

It is in stage 4 where knowledge turns into heart-felt conviction. This is a tough stage, often begun in young adulthood, when people start seeing outside the box and realize that there are other "boxes" of alternate values and understandings among those around them. They begin to critically examine their beliefs on their own and come to their own convictions. For many this is new appreciation for the Christian faith in which they were nurtured.

When struggling between Stage 3 and Stage 4, many youth appear to have fallen away, leaving others shaking their heads at this loss. This can be village thinking. A hundred years ago few young adults in a village ran into challenges to their faith. They accepted it and lived accordingly. In today's social culture Christian teens are surrounded daily with peers who live by other values and even mock those who go to church. The challenge now is to move beyond village culture. Adopting a vocabulary for struggle and the possibility of recovery is a very wise move for traditional churches.

Being given and raised in an identity by parents and church is good. But choosing that identity after struggle is even better for growth in faith and discipleship. Recognizing and encouraging such a choice involves a different approach to ministry.

Recognizing a Transforming Experience

About 4:30 p.m. on Saturday, September 2, 1970 James Loder, his wife and two daughters were on a New York highway heading in their camper north to Canada. They spotted a middle-aged woman standing near a disabled Oldsmobile with a flat tire and pulled off the road to help. He was trying to position the jack and had his head under the front looking for where to place it when a car, driven by a man asleep at the wheel, rammed the back of Olds and pushed it fifteen feet forward into the back of the camper, with James dragged along. Trapped with the front of the Olds on his chest, he called for help. Injuries included broken ribs, punctured lung and skin scrapes from head to foot and the tip of the thumb torn off. His wife, a "slight" woman, tried to help by lifting up on the bumper until she lost consciousness and was then surprised to see that the car had been lifted. She broke a vertebra in the effort.

Loder reports, "As I roused myself from under the car, a steady surge of life was rushing through me, carrying with it two solid assurances. First, I knew how deeply I felt love for those around me. The second assurance was that this disaster had a purpose. I never felt more conscious of the life that poured through me, nor more aware that this life was not my own."[35]

At that time James Loder was a junior faculty member of Princeton Theological Seminary, where he went on to became Professor of the Philosophy of Christian Education. Much of his academic career was devoted to understanding what happened in what he calls a "transforming moment" and how such moments emerge in the lives of many others. He calls it a "convicting experience." It was an encounter with the supernatural. It was an awakening of a very special kind not granted to all.

Theological Repression

One of Loder's discoveries is a survey result showing that about 80% of Presbyterian clergy and half of their lay constituency have had some such experiences. Yet seldom are these talked about. Loder calls this situation a "theological repression."

Theological repression is a good term for what happens in a church culture that is not open to God's supernatural interventions. Such culture has little room for recognizing the Holy Spirit's interventions in bringing any special motivation for ministry and in producing character-changing extraordinary fruit. In such a culture the Spirit part of the Trinity seems only partially known.

Gordon D. Fee tells about a student who said to him, "God the Father I understand, Christ the Son I know, but the Holy Spirit is a gray oblong blur." Fee goes on to observe that for many church communities the Spirit is kept in the creed, lest he become a vital—and perhaps threatening—part of the church's ongoing life. Thus in belief Protestants maintain their trinitarianism, but in practice many are thoroughgoing binitarians.[36]

Ignoring the third person is one reaction, in effect repressing what cannot be explained. A better response is to recognize, seek understanding and adjust one's view of God accordingly. We can learn to wait upon the Spirit, who can be full of surprises.

"Transformation" has become a buzz word in corporate as well as church cultures. Transformations are good. They represent changes that result in better performance for organizations and better living for individuals.

But true transformations are seldom. The word itself comes from Latin meaning to change forms. The Greek version we know as metamorphosis, what parents teach children about caterpillars who turn into butterflies. This is a thorough change. Personal transformations are usually dramatic and very memorable. They are quite different from step-by-step transitions. Most religious experiences are somewhere in between. These are still important to share. But transformational awakenings are especially important.

Reflections on a Transforming Moment.

We return to James Lober and his September 2, 1970 accident. Reflecting on it, he observes, "I never felt more conscious of the life that poured through me, nor more aware that this life was not my own."

He begins *The Transforming Moment* with his description of the accident and how this incident led him to a "convictional knowledge" of who he is in relation to God as experienced in a close brush with death. It was conviction beyond reason. Such stories are often told as an experience of conversion. Understanding this experience is important in order to avoid "an anti-intellectual rush of enthusiastic clichés." Such emotional enthusiasms are a symptom that theology has not been able "to supply understanding, comprehension and an adequate language for what takes place in these convicting moments of transformation.

Here are several more generalizations Loder offers about such transforming experiences.

- No one can know or comprehend the central meaning of a convicting experience from a standpoint outside of it. It is intensely personal.

- The validation of a word from God is uniformly established by God's initiative, not by generally recognized human procedures.

- A claim to having heard God's word may be falsified by human means but is finally and ultimately validated by God.

- Knowing—generally and convictionally—is first, foremost, and fundamentally an event. At the center is a non-rational intrusion of a convincing insight.

I would add the comment that such an *event* is really an *encounter* with Jesus Christ, like Paul had on the road to Damascus.

Stories of Spirit and Memory

There is growing recognition that communicating the Gospel is best done by telling stories. This is what Jesus did and this is what the four Gospels do. The Apostle Paul recognized that each believer in Corinth can tell a story of before and after their encounter with Christ. "You show that you are a letter from Christ, the result of our ministry, written not with ink but with the Spirit of the living God, not on tablets of stone but on tablets of human hearts" (2 Corinthians: 3: 3).

Good theory backs up this observation about the power of stories. It comes from John Shea, a master storyteller as well as theologian especially popular in Roman Catholic circles. He is also good at explaining the significance of storytelling for spirituality in the context of church.

Here are some highlights from his book *An Experience Named Spirit: Spirituality and Storytelling*.[37] Shea's two main concepts are Spirit and Memory.

Spirit is the Holy Spirit at work in so many lives and circumstances. Story is one of the primal expressions of the experience named Spirit, and Christian faith regularly retells its sacred stories. The great hope of every retelling is that the tale will powerfully intersect the life of the hearers so they will experience in some way the reality of Spirit.

Memory is accumulation of remembered rituals, espoused beliefs and theologies, enacted values and behaviors that are shared. Christians are People of Spirit and Memory whose soul is their living relationship with God, which is activated by the experience named Spirit. Memories are stockpiled as generation succeeds generation, and they are constantly in need of reform in order to be faithful to the living God at work in new generations. Traces of this Memory, like songs, worship, and buildings, have many different and very important functions, but only one ultimate purpose. They are expressions of the experience named Spirit and are meant to facilitate that experience for all who currently come into contact with the Gospel.

The goal of ministry, Shea says, is to bring together two sets of triggers of religiously significant experiences. One trigger is church and tradition. The second and more extensive set of triggers are the multiple life situations in which people find themselves. In situations of sickness and vitality, of questing for truth and struggling for justice, of loving and reconciling, of pondering the vastness of space and of traveling the inner, endless journey of the psyche, people come upon the reality of God. Such life situations seem to be the more traveled path to religious awareness today. The presence that people used to find in the dark back of Gothic churches they now claim they find in the bright light of the secular world.

A special sanctuary with high-quality finishings and maybe stained glass windows used to be a trigger for spiritual awareness for older generations. But this setting, like the back of Gothic churches, does not work so well for younger generations—the post- moderns—who work out their faith through engagement with the world around them. They are attracted to EPIC worship—Experiential, Participative, Image-driven and Communal, in the acronym proposed by Leonard Sweet.[38] This can happen easily in a gym.

What triggers religious experiences depends a lot on the upbringing of the adult. Ever since the collapse of the Sunday School movement several decades ago, most young adults now have a different set of triggers than their parents.

Understanding the Meaning of the Experience

John Shea uses a quote from T. S. Elliot, "We had the experience but missed the meaning." Men and women of today undergo events which, with the eyes of faith, are authored by the Spirit. But the religious significance of these events often goes unheralded. While the Spirit is the permeating energy of the experience, his work is not recognized. When the experience is seen in purely secular terms, then its God-power does not break into consciousness.

It is important that the telling of the experience be in story form. If we give only the pattern of experience, we cut short the process of personal appropriation of the experience through the story. Storytelling has a power of involvement and appreciation that the mere noting of patterns or the talking about experiences analytically does not have.

Here are some more nuggets:

- Psychology and sociology can *illuminate* what happened, but, in the last analysis, they cannot *determine* what happened. It becomes explicitly religious when the one with the experience judges it to be a time of contact with a transcendent otherness. Divine reality has made itself felt.

- The divine is not nakedly apprehended but intuited by what it is making happen.

- In the excesses and pretensions of the Spirit we look to the Memory of Jesus for direction and perspective. But when Memory threatens to alienate us from the depth of the present, we look to the Spirit to bring us life. Spirit and Memory are critical correctives.

- When we retain the message of the King but lose the feel for his presence, the passion of religious mission turns to dull obligation.

- Religious traditions die because they lose touch with their God. Religions usually degenerate in the end into a rationalistic theology, a formal morality and a ritualistic cult. Sometimes a religion which is nothing more has ceased to live.

- Within the Christian tradition many have deplored

this process of development and adaptation. For them every change has smacked of betrayal. Others have welcomed development. For them change is a sign of vitality.

Conversion or Awakening?

Telling your story, according to John Shea, is very important. Stories have to have words. What words are best?

Conversion stories are favored and well told in believer-baptizing churches in America, in contrast to infant-baptizing churches. Some, indeed, are of radical change from one way of life to a new life in Christ. How God does this can be fascinating. But many such stories are told by those who had grown up in a Christian community and at least passively confessed the faith. Then something happens and their faith takes on new meaning with energetic Christian living. Is that a conversion? Here is the place to explain why "awakening" is a better word for most major faith stories.

Conversion

Conversion is inadequate for three reasons. First, it does not cover people who have known from the beginning of memory that they are a child of the triune God. To imply they were not Christians until this special later experience denies the foundational understanding of God's grace applied by infant-baptizing churches.

Secondly, "conversion" does not set up the born again for subsequent peak religious experiences on their journey towards Christ likeness.

The life transformation called conversion is an attractive research topic for psychologists of religion. The *classic* paradigm is sudden conversion like that of Paul's initial encounter with

Christ. But there is a new *emerging* paradigm for research that recognizes gradual conversion. It has these characteristics: conversion occurs gradually; it is more rational than emotional; it is a process of self-realization; it is not permanent and may occur several times. No one experience is representative of all conversions.[39]

Thirdly, conversion is an inadequate translation for the word used in Scriptures. Those who talk about conversion experiences usually cite the Greek *metanoia*, which means literally "change of mind." Yet in all but one instance the NIV translates this word as "repentance." To repent means to be sorry, to regret past ways.

Is it better in ministry to focus on conversions or on repentance? Repentance is much the bigger concept and broader approach that applies to all who are seeking Christ. Where you are coming from is not as important as where you are now and where you are going. God cannot do much with someone who is full of him or herself. His Spirit can accomplish more with those who are sorry for their past sins and faulty allegiances.

Awakening

There has to be a better word than conversion to describe this life-long process of transformational steps on the way to becoming more like Christ. Let that word be "awakening." It is biblical. Paul tells the Romans to wake up from their slumber and to clothe themselves with the Lord Jesus Christ (5: 11). He tells the Thessalonians not to be like others who are asleep but be alert and self-controlled, putting on faith, love and hope (I: 5: 6-8). Is not this a call to awaken to more fruit of the Spirit?

There is a coherent theology behind this emphasis on awakening. The 17th century continental Pietists chose awakening as their key word for the renewal of life in Christ so much in need by nominal Christians and their churches at that time. They emphasized biological instead of traditional legal language and put a heavy emphasis on growth as God's work to make things new. Resurrection power was a key concept. The God who is good enough to justify persons is also powerful enough to change their lives.

The Apostle John ends his Gospel by telling us that Jesus did many other things beyond those he just reported. John observes, "If every one of them were written down, I suppose that even the whole world would not have room for the books that would be written." If those in that generation would fill a whole book, what would the book look like 20 centuries later, with 80 generations of billions of Christians telling their story of encounters with Jesus through his Word. Almost all of those are lost in history.

But we who are alive now can carry on the noble tradition by telling our stories, by witnessing personally to present generations. Join the parade. Tell your faith stories.

For you did not receive a spirit that makes you a slave again to fear, but you received the Spirit of sonship (by which we are) brought into the glorious freedom of the children of God.
Romans 8: 14, 21

CHAPTER 6
Modify Your Church Culture to Thrive Spiritually

On a recent Fall Saturday I and several others from church were pulling weeds in the yard of an elderly widow we had never met and who was not from our church. Two others were cleaning her basement. We were among 300 from church that went out on Servant Saturday morning to do just that—serve others in the community with no ulterior motive. Just finding enough work for that many was a major organizing project done by a staff member. She worked through the city government, whose staff identified mostly elderly in need of help. The mayor showed up after our breakfast to send us on the way. He seemed genuinely moved. It was a win-win for everybody involved.

What brought my church, Royal Redeemer Lutheran near Cleveland, to that Saturday morning? It was an outgrowth of staff discussions about new ways to accomplish our goal: To make and grow disciples. Our new logo featured three words: Connect, Belong, Thrive. We want to *connect* with many in our suburban community, purposely *include* them in our church community, and help all participants *thrive* in their spiritual life. The third—thrive—is the hardest.

This new effort aimed to develop a church culture that includes generous service to others. We knew generosity has to be a consistent theme in sermons. We highlighted the joy that comes from being generous to others. We knew this behavior has to be modeled by staff. We knew servant behavior is more likely to happen when opportunities are organized to do this with others. We were learning how to help participants thrive in just this one aspect of spiritual growth.

Thrive is indeed the new frontier for mission-minded congregations. Helping church participants not just grow but really thrive in their personal spiritual life is the challenge for churches wanting to do better in their ministry in the future.

Thirty or so years ago saw a movement among conservative Protestant churches called Church Growth. The emphasis was on numeric growth of participants in a congregation by learning from churches that indeed had grown, some to tens of thousands of attendees on a weekend. One observation was that congregations needed to make a conscious decision to grow and then remove barriers. In effect they changed their church culture to more openness to the unchurched. Seeker services became popular, aimed beyond the members at visitors. This intent to *connect* with others brought significant changes to the church culture of many congregations.

Parallel was the small group movement of the 1980s and 90s. In the suburban environment it is hard for one person to relate to hundreds of others they do not know with a sense *belonging*. Thus many church leaders today strive to foster small group interaction for Bible study and mutual encouragement. This effort makes a lot of sense but in our experience is hard to accomplish and sustain. Yet the result is so important that we keep plugging away at making small groups a part of our church culture.

There is growing evidence that the movement today is toward *thriving* in the Spirit. In Chapter 2 I featured how the Spirit-oriented Pentecostal movement keeps growing worldwide while the strongly Word-oriented traditional church bodies are in decline. One study of a thousand Protestant congregations identified the sixteen "most vibrant, spiritually alive congregations" they knew of. By my assessment of their websites, three fifths of those are highly Spirit-oriented.[40]

Another large-scale research effort identified "Passionate Spirituality" as one of the most important characteristics of healthy, growing congregations.[41] In discussions I have had with leaders in traditional church bodies, someone will inevitably observe that "passionate" and their tradition are an oxymoron—a contradiction. This is a sure formula for decline.

Think about it! What unchurched person would want to become part of a congregation where participation does not seem to make a difference in the lives of those involved, at least from their outsider perspective? To state the case differently, why would they want to participate in a congregation where most do not appear to be thriving spiritually?

Decide to Thrive Spiritually

One of the observations from the Church Growth movement was that in order to grow numerically a congregation has to decide consciously to grow and then remove barriers that stand in the way. The same can be said for congregations that want to thrive spiritually. This happens best with a conscious decision to cultivate soil for the Holy Spirit and to remove church-culture barriers that block the Holy Spirit from doing his renewing work among those gathered as the congregation. One thing is certain. Greater spiritually is not going to happen by doing the same old things the same old ways among the same people.

I *am not* advocating imitation of Pentecostals. Basic spiritual temperaments have to be respected. Protestants from northern European cultures (home of Lutherans, Calvinists and Anglicans) seem to have inherent resistance to strong emotional displays. I once observed a two-hour Pentecostal service where the pastor, knowing I was there, pulled out all the stops for emotional displays. Feeling emotionally abused, I was eager to leave when the end finally came.

I *am* advocating that congregations get back to basic spirituality. Jesus wants us to worship in spirit and truth. The truth part is largely under human control through what is preached and taught. But truth without spirit is barren. Objective truth needs to become subjective, and that is the Spirit's work. Paul wants us to become Christ-like, and this certainly involves righteous behavior. But the specifics of the behavior are not as important as the heart-condition for doing them. Changing hearts should be the objective, and this is the Spirit's work.

Paul understood the human heart as the workplace for the Spirit sent by God. He tells the Romans that it is with their hearts that they believe and are justified (10:10), and that God poured out his love into their hearts by the Holy Spirit (5:5), who knows our hearts better than we do (8: 27). He tells the Ephesians he wishes the Father's love may strengthen them with power through the Spirit in their inner being, so that Christ may dwell in their hearts through faith (3:17). Softening hearts is the Spirit's specialty.

Since the Holy Spirit is involved, the results are unpredictable. What works for some does not bring the same result for others. It is much easier to deal with heads and teach for knowledge. The time-honored, village-church assumption is that head knowledge turns into heart conviction. For many, this did happen, but often only in a superficial way.

In today's urban areas, however, Christian beliefs and values are under constant assault. Deeper conviction comes through experiences of struggle. Churches can welcome such struggle among participants as the workplace for the Spirit. They can learn how to adapt their support to individual circumstances. But first needs to come a commitment to follow the Spirit's unpredictable ways.

There is much talk about spirituality in our American culture these days. Definitions vary widely and can include almost anything beyond material existence. But recognize this: If you are talking spirituality but are not focused on the Holy Spirit, then you are not talking biblical Christian spirituality. Part of consciously developing a church culture for thriving in the Spirit is to get back to Bible basics.

The Holy Spirit and Church Organization

I had invited seminary staff from my area for a barbeque on the deck of our home. Unlike many other men, I don't enjoy this ritual. Soon after I put the chicken pieces on the grill, a flame burst out and got bigger from the fat drippings on the hot coals. I figured I could control that by lowering the hood and reducing the size of the air vents. It worked. The flame went away. But when I looked again ten minutes later there was not only no flame but also no heat. I can't remember what we did for the chicken part of the meal, which obviously did not go as planned. But that evening I recognized and have not forgotten this event as a metaphor for dealing with the Spirit in a church.

A flame is one of the two classic symbols for the Holy Spirit who came upon the apostles at Pentecost. The other is sound like the blowing of a violent wind. Jesus himself blessed wind as a metaphor for the Spirit at work. He explained to Nicodemus, ""The wind blows wherever it pleases. You hear its sound but you cannot tell where it comes from or where it is going. So it is with everyone born of the Spirit." The analogy works better in the original Greek, where the word for wind, *pneuma*, is the same as for the Spirit. We have it today in English when we talk about *pneumatic* tools that are driven by air pressure, like the hand tool used to take wheels of a car in a tire shop. The Spirit is that pneumatic power in Christian lives.

The problem comes when Jesus explained that you cannot tell where the wind is coming from or where it is going. Such wind is unpredictable. So is the Holy Spirit. We humans have limited tolerance for the unpredictable. We like to have reliable control over what will happen in the future.

Rather than risk a burst of damaging flame in church life, we prefer to limit the amount of oxygen of the Holy Spirit getting into what we are doing together as a fellowship. Experienced grillers would have known how better to handle my crude attempt to control the chicken barbeque. Experienced church leaders can learn how to better control the Spirit's work without putting out his flame.

Max Lucado offers a helpful image for how to welcome the Spirit into our lives and fellowship. Living in Texas, he appreciated the cool air of his writing room. He cannot take credit for the compressor. It came with the mortgage. But he also has to open the vents in the room. "I did not install the 'air makers,' but I did open the 'air blockers.' Cool air fills the house because the vents are open."[42]

Change the reference point to Ohio and to a furnace rather than an air compressor. The analogy gets even better. Do you want more of the warmth of the Spirit? Open up the air blockers.

Face Leadership Fears

Look for the oxygen of the Holy Spirit in the motivations of individual believers. Expect participants to contribute to the common good what the Spirit moves them to do in their different unique ways. But is not this a prescription for chaos as participants get in each other's way heading in different directions? Certainly this can happen—in the absence of wise leadership. Thus Paul emphasized the second part of the Spirit's movement to grow within each the fellowship-building fruit of love, patience, trust, kindness, gentleness and self-control—all of which are basic to working together peacefully. So, yes. Spirit-inflamed believers can bring stress into a church community. But with cultivation of a congregation's soil the Spirit can also work out the solution through character changes that bring unity. The result can be a very exciting church community that furthers the kingdom of God in the lives of those they touch.

Protestant congregations today should recognize two kinds of fears that can drive their decision making. One is having so much spiritual energy that the fellowship bursts apart from all the activity. The other is having so little spiritual energy that their church fades away. The first is hardly a realistic fear for the many withering congregations today. They would do better to run the risk of letting in more of the Spirit and his special energy.

Fresh energy usually happens when the Spirit brings in believers new to the fellowship and with a different perspective. In my church plant three families from Pentecostal/charismatic background were active for several years and then left. Meanwhile they modeled for us an exciting prayer life that still characterizes the congregation.

In so many ways the Apostle Paul was personally fearless in his mission work. He recognized that "you did not receive a spirit that makes you a slave again to fear, but you received the Spirit of sonship (by which we are) brought into the glorious freedom of the children of God" (Romans 8: 14, 21). Congregations can learn to reduce slavery to fear with the freedom inherent in Paul's understanding of their life together.

A major step toward more freedom in church life is to become more tolerant of differences in the spiritual journey of participants and to loosen expectations of the one best way. This means reducing dependence on traditions as the guide to what will be done in the future and being open to new approaches. To do so means resisting the urge to solve problems by making more rules. Take it from a specialist in organizational behavior that tighter organization is not necessarily better organization when it reduces flexibility to adapt to changes happening in its environment.

Loosen Up a Traditional Church Organization

Traditional congregations that want to foster the work of the Spirit in their midst will need to consider changes in their church culture. This is especially true for congregations that carry on the old culture of village churches.

Consider some options for how we organize our *relationship*s and our patterns of *communication* together. Both are matters of church culture. A culture is an integrated pattern of knowledge, beliefs and behaviors that determines what is learned and transmitted to future generations. The emphasis here is on behaviors. The same beliefs can shape different behaviors. In the last chapter I will explore how a culture of behavior usually trumps beliefs. To change a culture you have to change behaviors.

Patterns of Relationships

One time-tested way to reduce conflict in a village is to

separate the leader from the rest, that is, to recognize clergy as distinct from the laity. The really important religious activities are reserved for only the clergy to do, who have years of schooling and come from outside the village. The role for the rest is to support by praying and paying for the real ministry.

The Apostle Paul would have had a hard time understanding this way of organizing. He would certainly agree that spiritual leaders are important, but would expect believers to emerge in these roles through proven ability that would affirm a special calling by the Spirit. From the village perspective, Paul's understanding of everyone being gifted by the Spirit for a specific function in the body would make no sense. No wonder his emphasis disappeared for centuries.

In my church plant, one of the leaders was well respected for his wisdom. I learned much from him about discipling others. One of the other leaders complained that Norm just wanted to be pastor. My reaction was, God bless him. How can I help?

Patterns of Communicating

Part of organizing a congregation can be seen in patterns of communication. In a village it is almost all one-way, from the pastor to the people, who are assumed to have little of value to share. Their responses are fully scripted and their songs carefully selected from songs composed in the past. If worship is to be in spirit and truth, the safer approach is to emphasize carefully controlled truth even at the expense of spirit.

I am advocating story telling about personal encounters with the Spirit. This approach stands in contrast to the pattern of traditional churches. The old assumption is that lay people have little of spiritual value to offer. They are to receive insights, not give. But encouraging them to share how the Holy Spirit influenced their lives can open our eyes to how the Spirit works.

Such sharing can prepare us for how, in God's grace, we, too, can grow under the influence of the Spirit. It is important that their stories be told in ways appropriate to the situation. This calls for reliance on the fruit of wisdom that the Spirit can provide.

The leadership challenge is to organize more ways in which such sharing can happen. Some churches do provide time in public worship for testimonials. There is little precedent in mainline churches, and participants usually do not have experience for telling their story well. One way to introduce faith stories is to have them video-taped and then edited into a more compact form. But then someone has to spend time on the project. This can be an opportunity for the leaders to pray that the Father send his Holy Spirit to motivate someone to step forward for this specialized video ministry.

We have to assume that constantly evolving communication technology is part of God's ongoing creation. The more effective communication this makes possible in itself can provide more opportunity for the Spirit to touch lives. Learning how to use such technology can become one more challenge for church leaders who want to turn around decline.

Offering New Church Experiences the Spirit Can Use

A new word has emerged to describe some religious experiences that are beyond most mainline Protestant traditions. These are "threshold" experiences. If you like a fancier word, anthropologists speak of "liminality." A threshold is a sill at the bottom of a doorway into a different room. These experiences view a familiar truth or relationship from the fresh perspective of standing in a different doorway.

Short-term mission trips to a very different culture of another country are great threshold experiences for many participants. A lot of congregations today do one-week trips in support of ongoing work of a Christian church or community in a less developed country. "Life changing" is often the reaction to observing the poverty and the faith of these fellow Christians. "Church changing" happens as well to congregations from which a team goes. They bring back new enthusiasm for mission that stimulates others to look for ways to reach out. My mission interest has as much to do with church renewal at home as it has with impacting lives of others to whom we are in mission.

Week end renewal events can be another threshold experience for those involved. Precedent is set by programs variously called Cursillo, Walk to Emmaus, Via de Christo or Faith Alive in different denominations. Those programs are now in decline because of difficulties recruiting participants to spend three or four days away from home, spouse and family. "Celebrate Journeys in Christ" is a version we worked on. It shortens the format to a Friday evening and all day Saturday. This happens at the church so that participants can go home for the night. Key to the experience is having leaders give a short personal testimony, a faith-witness about what God has done in changing their lives. These stories become the basis for small group discussions. The discussions help stimulate in participants a reflection on what God has done in their lives. Their stories, in effect, become a personal witness by testimony, which gives hope and encouragement to others, many of whom had no idea what was happening spiritually in the lives of fellow church members they have known for years. We ask participants to plot out on a graph paper the line that would reflect the ups and downs of their spiritual life over the years—their personal spiritual journey.

Both kinds of threshold experience give expression to what Paul called the many-faceted wisdom of God (Ephesians 3: 10). A facet is a face or surface. Diamonds are cut to have many facets that reflect light in different directions, giving the "bling" to a diamond ring—the more facets the more bling. Preachers have long practiced proclaiming different perspectives on Christ's life and work, like seeing him as shepherd, bread of life, vine, or living water. These many facets are held up for view by those sitting in the pews. Another way to change the perception moves people out of the pews into very different settings, like someone's living room, or a mission trip, or a renewal weekend.

Christian church cultures have changed dramatically over the centuries as churches, under the Spirit's influence, adapted to new countries and changing circumstances. Those that did not change became mostly footnotes in church history. Those who want to insist on maintaining their traditions today might want to ask which tradition they choose, because long-established church bodies have changed some of their dominant traditions with every generation over the centuries. Change can be good. This is what the Holy Spirit specializes in.

Be Open To Supernatural Interventions

One of the stories we told at church concerns a ten-year old girl who was shopping with her Mom on a Saturday evening. Her speech became garbled. Fearing the worst, Mom took her to the hospital emergency room. She had had a brain aneurism. Physicians told the mother to prepare for the worst. If the girl survived she would not talk or walk. We prayed for her in the Sunday services. At about 11:00 am a large group gathered to pray some more. That afternoon the nurse reported that the girl woke up about 11:00 am and talked and walked. She has turned into a beautiful young woman who regularly attends our services with her mother. Thank God for answered prayer.

Was this a miracle? Or was it just an unusual coincidence, perhaps based on a misdiagnosis?

The central issue of this book is whether God interacts with people in supernatural ways today. Traditional mainline churches confess that the third person of the Trinity is active in general, but for all practical purposes they have no expectations of the Spirit's supernatural work in lives and churches today. I have kept the focus on observable changes in the inner motivations and feelings of believers. What about changes visible in the bodily condition of a person—changes for which there is no natural explanation? In other words, does God do healing miracles today?

Part of my spiritual journey has been to gain confidence that indeed the supernatural God of the Bible can and does intervene in otherwise unexplainable ways now, as he did in Biblical times. This journey took me to Nigeria as part of a medical team in the crusade of Uma Ukpai, Miracle Worker. At home I did what I called Prayer for Healing services at which a leg lengthening happened. I am impressed with a pastor colleague in our very traditional, "miracles-ceased" Lutheran church body who was very ill, went to a Benny Hinn service, was restored to full health, and now he and his wife have their own healing ministry. At a retreat I heard a hospital pathologist, who reads the initial biopsy and the one just before surgery, remark that indeed cancers do disappear "more often than you think." Much of what I learned about prayer for healing came from a retired, otherwise traditional Presbyterian pastor from Canton, Ohio, Rev. Donald Bartow.

In my own research through a random survey of 366 Lutheran pastors I found that 75% had experienced or witnessed a miracle, defined as an unusual event for which there is no natural explanation. Yet in our church culture we never talk about this.

The issue was settled in my mind years ago. Doubts about the supernatural Spirit's involvement in natural affairs, like doubts about the special inspiration of Scriptures, have largely gone away. I attribute this to the Holy Spirit's work on me.

It certainly makes possible much greater appreciation of the Apostle Paul's robust theology of the Spirit at work in churches today—a theology that gives powerful purpose for the work of Christian congregations.

Actually coming to the conclusion that God can indeed be supernaturally involved in human affairs should logically lead into a whole change in world view, something that is indeed now happening in Western culture. Let seminary professor Luther Halverson explain what happened to him personally when he recognized the results of intercessory prayer for others.

This cultural revolution suggest a shift in one's mode of being and doing that so radically reverses, upsets, and disorients that it amounts to a conversion or a passage through Alice's mirror. In it the same reality is seen, the same data observed, but everything is different, perhaps even opposite.

Although the empirical and experiential are part of the data reviewed with new eyes, I believe that the change has more to do with vision than analysis, serendipity than calculation, the Holy Spirit than prescribed ritual and dogma.[43]

It is easy to disprove a negative. All you have to do is find one exception. The negative at hand is that God does not intervene in supernatural ways. After years of inquiry my conclusion is that this negative proposition is false. Evidence keeps mounting that God does intervene supernaturally.

Develop a Spiritual Counter Culture in Churches Today

The kind of Spirit-oriented church culture that I envision would be counter to three other cultures Protestants encounter today: 1) the classic Reformation teaching that miracles ceased in the New Testament, 2) the emotion-laden Pentecostal crusades seen on television, 3) university culture with a one dimensional view of reality.

1) Counter to "No More Miracles"

The Reformation of 500 years ago happened against the backdrop of widespread Medieval superstition and belief in miraculous power of shrines and relics. Against such beliefs, the very rational John Calvin taught that "Those miraculous powers and manifest workings, which were dispensed by the laying on of hands, have ceased; and they have rightly lasted only for a time."[44] We are to look for the miraculous in the everyday creative ways that God provides for our health and well-being. Thus supernatural interventions ceased after Christianity was established in the first century.

Luther was somewhat more open minded but not much. He prayed for his colleague Philip Melanchthon who was at the brink of death, so that Melanchthon later wrote how he was recalled from death to life by divine power. Luther laid out an order of service based on James 5 for a pastor to use to help an individual named John Korner. But little came of this. The result was the very same cessation assumptions in the Lutheran church doctrine and history I experienced. The bottom line for traditional churches of the Reformation was: Don't expect supernatural interventions in any practical way today.[45]

The most difficult position to maintain, it seems to me, is this cessationist view that God could intervene now like he did in Bible times, but he chooses not to do so today. There is certainly no Biblical evidence for this perspective. It is not a logically coherent position. It has the consequence of depriving many Word-oriented churches of the increased spiritual power that comes from greater openness to the working of the Holy Spirit.

2) Counter to "Do Special Things To Get God Moving"

Vineyard Pastor Ken Blue provided valuable perspective for my journey of understanding miraculous interventions. He joins many other mature Pentecostals in warning against what can be called a "faith formula." This is a view that if you just know enough, repent enough, pray enough you will get special blessings and gifts of the Spirit, including healing. He notes that this view largely accounts for the volume of noise and emotionalism at some healing meetings—a frenzy they think will get God moving.[46]

This intent to get God moving on our schedule by our actions can be a form of work righteousness for salvation, where getting right with God depends on what I do, not on his initiative. The function of a living faith is not to get specified results. It is to trust God in his love to take the initiative to give what is good for us. This is grace in action. This grace needs to stay central in a church culture fashioned for our times.

I have worked out for myself that miracles do happen but are rare, perhaps one percent of the time. Some observers estimate 2-4 percent. But even one percent is enough to demonstrate the possibility. Might one percent be enough to change a world view in general and ministry practices in particular? To me it is enough to warrant changing a church's culture to more openness to the Spirit's movement among those gathered.

3) Counter To One-Dimensional University Culture

What kind of reception can you expect if you share a miracle experience? You will probably be heard with interest. Sociologist Robert Wuthnow in his study of spirituality in America reports recent national poll results that find 83 percent of Americans agree miracles are performed even today by the power of God. Another study reported that 68 percent of Americans definitely or probably believe in miracles. Even among people who seldom or never attend religious services, a majority think miracles probably happen. Where you will find pushback is among people with graduate degrees, only 18 percent of which definitely believe in miracles.⁴⁷

University culture is distinct. But this is changing, according to Craig S. Keener (Ph.D. Duke University). In his 2011 two volume publication *Miracles*, he reviewed the credibility of miracles from all possible viewpoints, summarizing issues and citing cases.

Keener notes how philosophers of science acknowledge that even fundamental principles—presuppositions taken for granted—must be open to revision in the light of further discovery. Such paradigm shifts become revolutions in world view, in ways of conceptualizing the universe. Theories succeed by proving more persuasive than their competitors, but once they become dominant they are displaced only with difficulty. Keener points out that academic politics can play a role in their resilience. Thus some resistance to new extra-normal claims from around the world is not surprising "though the quantity of these claims is now becoming overwhelming." He observes,

(Academic) consensus does not determine truth, and many statements of consensus are premature in any case. Some older modern theologians like Bultmann declared that "mature" modern people do not believe in miracles, and that "no one can or does seriously maintain" the NT worldview. Those following such an approach can examine miracle account's theological and social functions while dismissing their historical foundations. Yet even as some theologians were demythologizing the Bible to make it relevant for an anti-supernaturalist audience, belief in miracles was rising among the Western public.⁴⁸

Post-Modern Opportunities

The irony is that, in contrast to the modernist pace setters, younger generations have become post-modern. The term is vague but in general describes a movement in reaction to the assumed certainty of scientific efforts to explain reality. Post moderns are typically not ready to accept the institutional church and its teachings developed over centuries. But they are open to a reality beyond what can be proven empirically. Miracles and supernatural power are not dismissed out of hand.

Paul Prather summarizes,

"We Westerners, particularly, are becoming more open about the possibility of divine intervention today because the Enlightenment paradigm on which we so long depended has failed us miserably.... At the same time certain breakthroughs in the theoretical sciences such as physics have suggested that our cosmos is not the closed precise, predictable universe that Newtonian scientists assumed, but rather that it contains quirky, unpredictable agents and events."[49]

A growing dissatisfaction with a one-dimensional view that recognizes only the material world can be seen most clearly in former Communist countries, like China. There Christianity is growing rapidly. Most of that growth is occurring in churches that have high expectations of the Holy Spirit.

For someone of my generation with a graduate university background, this openness among the educated to supernatural interventions is a big deal. It calls for a two-dimensional view of the world that sets aside old certainties and offers new opportunities for daily living. For churches, readiness to recognize that the Holy Spirit can indeed empower ministry and improve relationships should have major implications for how ministry is done.

To put this most dramatically, if there is credible evidence of one true miracle—a special event for which there is no natural explanation—that should be enough logically to demolish an old one-dimensional world view.

The culture of a congregation usually does change from

generation to generation, even if only a little. Influences come from many directions. Open up your congregation to ideas and emphases of more Spirit-oriented congregations, starting with those closest to your tradition. Be willing to listen to insights and values of the young generation of post-moderns. Your future may well depend on new ways of appreciating the Holy Spirit's work today.

Come, let us rebuild the wall of Jerusalem and we will no longer be in disgrace. I also told them about the gracious hand of my God upon me and what the king had said to me. They replied, "Let us start rebuilding."
Nehemiah 2: 18

CHAPTER 7
Change the Behavior To Change the Culture

Recent decades have seen new forms of competition force a sorting out in traditional ways of doing business, running schools and staffing the military. Cheaper goods from abroad put price pressures on American manufacturers, leading to downsizing, sending jobs off shore and to adopting more responsive organization structures. The internet is reducing sales in retail establishments and driving newspaper and magazines out of existence. Wide-spread dissatisfaction with educational attainments of grade and high schools is forcing a new performance-based school culture. With no draft and ongoing wars, military forces had to adopt new ways to attract recruits and retain veterans. The new Army has been forced to change its old ways.

In short, most businesses and organizations in American society have faced increased competition and the need to change their culture for how things are done. Just about anyone over 25 can describe changes they have seen and how they personally have adapted.

Churches face the same social forces today: more

competition and higher expectations. More competition comes not only in the form of neighboring bigger churches with more program offerings, more sophisticated communication, and better facilities, but also in the presence of many more alternative ways to spend Sunday morning, like youth sporting events. Higher expectations turn into loss of loyalty and greater readiness to go someplace else when "this church doesn't meet my needs." Mainline Protestant churches in America had grown used to depending on loyalty to sustain membership and ministries. There is much less tolerance now for poor performance, especially with worship and sermons that fall short of engaging the participants.

Many churches are apparently resigning themselves to the inevitable withering that comes with loss of younger generations. Some pastors hope the end is far enough in the future to see them through to retirement.

A better response to this higher bar for congregations that want to remain healthy and effective is to become less reliant on tradition and more intentional about what they are trying to accomplish. Usually moving in that direction necessitates changing a congregation's inherited church culture.

A "hard" environment, by the way, is not uniform across American society. The "soft" environment will hold longer for churches in rural areas and small towns where social relationships are more stable and participants are more willing to adjust their expectations. In those circumstances decline will be from greater migration of youth to the big cities for more opportunities.

It is suburbia where the performance level needs to be increased because of more competition. Mobility is greater and fewer church participants know each other from encounters beyond the congregation. Shared memory is decreasing.

The harder environment means that the status quo of many congregations will not hold long.

The best response to this harder environment and the decrease of social support for churches is to go back to spiritual basics. This means to deliberately develop a more effective Holy Spirit church culture.

Recognizing a Church Culture

Anyone who has done church shopping knows the feeling of entering a worship service and feeling energized. It may be hard to figure out why, but the culture comes across as attractive. The opposite is to enter a service and feel the energy draining away. The reason why may be hard to identify, too. But as in so much of life, first impressions mean a lot.

Many church leaders and members would claim that such judgments are unfair because these observers do not appreciate the depth of what has been offered. They should learn first, and then decide. That may have worked in previous generations when so many felt obligated to be part of a church, or to say it differently, felt guilty if they were not. But that sense of obligation is increasingly hard to find in 21st century America. If people are looking for a church home, they want something positive out of the experience right from the beginning.

One small example would be a congregation's attitude towards C and E Christians, who come only on Christmas and Easter. The faithful tend to look down on such "visitors," and their attitude expresses itself in aloofness and stray comments. A mission-minded church, on the other hand appreciates these two opportunities to deliver a worship experience that will draw them back. Laying on guilt, as many historic churches do, may be counter-productive for drawing someone closer to Christ in that congregation. Church cultures of the future will focus on offering opportunities for personal benefit.

The dictionary definition of a culture is an integrated pattern of *knowledge, beliefs* and *behaviors* that determines what is learned and transmitted to future generations. Most congregations today can tell you what they know and believe, but few are aware of how their behaviors form a distinctive church culture. For trying to figure out why their ways are not transferring well to their young, the first place to look is at the behaviors their culture models. Often a younger generation sees what is or is not being done that the elders are not even aware of.

You can describe a church culture with answers to questions like these:

- When someone not from the congregation observes a Sunday service, what mood would he or she pick up?

- When someone inquires, "Tell me about your church," what stories are told?

- How many young families and children are participating?

- What do participants expect to happen during the worship?

- Who shares leadership of the church with the pastor?

- Who gets recognized and affirmed, and for what achievements?

- Does the church have clear direction for the future, and how widely is this affirmed among members?

- What is the level of creativity and enthusiasm among the participants?

- What does the condition of the physical facility tell about the values of members and leaders?

- How are decisions made, deferred, or delayed?
- Does the church talk mostly about the past or the future?

These are just a few lead questions to focus attention on who the people are, how they interact and behave, what they value the most. All this is in contrast to what is said or written about their intentions and motivations.

One summer I was chaplain at a county juvenile detention center. I thought we would get our Sunday worship off to a good start by singing the rousing "A Mighty Fortress is Our God." I still remember pianist's puzzled look and the first strange chords. It took only a few measures for me to figure out this Lutheran standard was not going anywhere. Time to switch to "Holy, Holy, Holy," which was played with gusto. I was that naïve about how church cultures differ. That naïve many Christian leaders are today about the limitations of the church culture they are used to.

Christian Schwarz is a contemporary German theologian and church researcher. He offers a framework for recognizing and describing key church dimensions in his Natural Church Development Survey. It consists of 91 statements that assess how often a participant does or observes specific behaviors. The result is an assessment of an individual congregation's church culture. The eight characteristics are: leadership, ministry, spirituality, structures, worship service, small groups, evangelism and relationships.[50]

Schwarz makes no pretense to be objective about what these qualities should look like in a healthy, effective Christian congregation. He presents an adjective in front of each quality:

Empowering leadership　　Gift-oriented ministry
Passionate spirituality　　Inspiring worship service

Functional structures   Holistic small groups
Need-oriented evangelism Loving relationships

Any congregation today can use this questionnaire to understand better the strengths and weaknesses of their specific church culture. It is available through Church Smart Resources at www.churchsmart.com.

Develop An Alive-in-the-Spirit Church Culture

Of these eight qualities, four have been the subject of this book: passionate spirituality, gift-oriented ministry, empowering leadership and loving relationships. As those improve, so will a fifth characteristic: inspiring worship services.

The seven preceding chapters have laid out steps toward developing a Holy Spirit culture. These are:

1. Regularly ask, seek and knock that the Father send his Holy Spirit, as he promises always to do.

2. Pray for the Spirit to come at specific times in specific circumstances.

3. Pause to recognize when such prayer has been answered with a Spirit encounter. Name it as such.

4. Share this encounter with a friend, a group of friends, and under the right circumstances with the larger congregation.

5. Work to arrange times and situations where suitable encounter stories can be told and discussed in the congregation. Aim toward including two to five minute personal testimonies into worship services.

6. Study in depth Paul's teachings on the gifts and fruit of the Spirit and their relevancy to church life today.

7. Do sermon series on the work of the Holy Spirit.

8. Identify remnants of village-church culture in the practices of your congregation. Discuss what, if anything, to do about them.

9. Recognize and discuss the differing spiritual temperaments of those in the congregation.

10. Learn how better to cultivate the soil of your church's life together to become a better host for the Holy Spirit.

11. Make time for heartfelt repentance.

12. Tell more exciting spiritual journey stories from the Bible, church history and contemporary Christians, also those in other lands.

13. Develop categories to describe different stages of a believer's growth in faith and grace.

14. Discuss whether your congregation focuses more on the past accomplishment or on future progress toward improved ministry to others. Consider where you are in the balance between Spirit and Memory.

15. Talk more openly about miracles otherwise not explainable that you have experienced or witnessed. Discuss the influence of the university one-dimensional world view.

16. Discuss how to start movement toward becoming more of a Holy Spirit church culture in your congregation.

A Few Principles About Culture Change

The reason to change a church's culture is so that the congregation can do its ministries more effectively in the future. Leading a culture change is challenging work.

In business the culture of a corporation is a huge topic for management. Sophisticated systems are used to analyze the culture present in any business or organization. The intent is to bring changes to that culture in order to increase productivity or some other outcome necessary for the organization's continued success. Usually increased competition calls the future into doubt and provides the incentive to make changes.

For churches, too, increased competition and decline provide the main incentive to understand and change church cultures. In the 1950s all Christian churches and their cultures were doing well in terms of planting new churches and growing in membership and attendance. This is not so anymore for mainline churches and increasingly for many Evangelical churches. Recognizing that the future is in doubt for many congregations can give incentive to assess the culture they inherited and to consider change.

Here are some principles from corporate culture change that are applicable to churches.

1. Changing an organization's culture is anxiety provoking. Edgar H. Schein authored the most popular textbook on organization culture and leadership, *Organizational Culture and Leadership*.[51] It is still used in business schools. He explains, The culture "provides its members with a basic sense of identity and defines the values that provide self-esteem. Cultures tell their members who they are, how to behave toward each other and how to feel good about themselves. Recognizing these critical functions makes us aware why 'changing' culture is so anxiety provoking."

   If these basic functions are true in a business, think how much more they apply to a church, which is all about providing basic identity and values and moral basis for behavior. No wonder change is difficult for churches.

Approach the remodeling of a church culture with caution.

2. A second principle is that strong leadership is needed to change an organizational culture. Without strong leadership to challenge current ways, congregations will settle back into what is familiar and comfortable. The key leader, of course, is the pastor. Effective change has to involve other leaders, but it is the pastor who decides what to feature and functionally has veto power over how much emphasis will be placed on other initiatives. Pastors typically have their core expertise in the ways of the old culture. Few are prepared to negotiate changes to something they themselves have little experience with. Many do not even consider themselves leaders to begin with. A question in any church is whether the pastor is up to the challenge. The job is less difficult if other leaders are ready to understand and support.

3. Culture change inevitably brings conflict between those who like the old and those espousing the new. By personality, most pastors are inclined to avoid conflict if possible. To lead change necessitates skills in handling conflict as part of managing changes in a church.

4. Leaders have to earn the right to be followed in new behaviors. In Schein's words, "Whatever is proposed will only be perceived as what the leader wants. Until the group has taken some joint action and together observed the outcome, there is not as yet a shared basis for determining whether what the leader wants will turn out to be valid." Some sort of success for new ways is crucial, even in a church.

5. Culture arises through shared experiences of success. It makes sense to earn credibility by starting with relatively small changes that are easy to do and are welcomed by almost all. Negotiating these easy changes will build trust.

6. Culture trumps vision. So declares Samuel Chand. Vision is about *ideas*. Culture is *behavior*. Culture change is all about turning new ideas into new actions that past behaviors would resist.

In short, until words turn into successful actions, not much will change in a church culture. Preaching a new emphasis is a good start. But until it results in action, persistence on that theme can turn into nagging that annoys more than motivates. In most cases, who needs to initiate the action? It is the pastor or leader who wants the change. Putting words into action usually takes organizational skills in arranging opportunities to express the desired behaviors.

Sometimes a growth spurt in a congregation is preceded by an "igniter" event. This is an event, often not planned, that allowed the congregation to experience success, which brought about new energy and openness to change. I am aware of one congregation that took on a service project of cleaning up the city park nearby. A TV crew came to interview them and produced a segment on the evening news. With this visible success the leaders were then ready to put more energy into exploring new ideas for ministry.

Where To Start Changing a Church Culture

A culture has three components. If a church's culture is no longer functioning well, is the problem that their culture has insufficient *knowledge*? Or are their *beliefs* poorly expressed? Or are they perhaps emphasizing the wrong kind of *behavior*?

Knowledge

The easiest part of a church culture to deal with is the knowledg*e* base. Maybe they don't know they are dying or that God is still alive and active throughout the world. It is easy to gather data to show where a congregation is failing and to describe what it should be doing. Denominational officials sometimes try this approach, proclaiming with alarm, in the case of my church body, that a huge proportion of congregations have not added more than one new member in the previous several years. What does this accomplish? Not much beyond making these many congregations feel guilty, unappreciated and even angry. In general, guilt seldom produces innovative new ways of meeting a challenge.

A ministry colleague tried to set a new direction by bringing in guest speakers to show how congregations in general can become self-centered and dysfunctional. Long-time members inferred the pastor did not appreciate them and rebelled against his contemporary worship efforts. He had to leave. Additional knowledge itself seldom is a vehicle of change. More important is to get the knowledge hooked up to beliefs and behaviors of a specific congregation of people. The hooking together is the leadership challenge. Culture change does not happen in general. It takes place when behaviors are changed step by step.

Beliefs and Values

Then how about changing a church's beliefs? Protestant churches are typically all about beliefs, at least the type that get expressed as doctrine. To understand all those differing doctrinal emphases requires going back into church history to understand issues that arose among Christians, usually in a given country in a specific century. Try to explain the beliefs that distinguish Southern, Northern or General Baptists without explaining a lot of their histories, like the Civil War. Most pastors are highly concerned about teachings and work hard to explain their truthfulness. Most members are less interested in the specifics; their values are much more pragmatic.

When I did my doctoral dissertation on pastors as organizational leaders, I visited and interviewed fifty-six suburban pastors of mainline denominations. One overall impression gained from looking at bulletin boards and publicity is that they all showed similar church cultures of events, groups, social activities. The names differed, but the expectations were about the same. Although Presbyterians, Lutherans, Episcopalians, Methodists and United Church of Christ have different belief emphases, they were all doing roughly the same things.

Consider this as evidence that distinctive church beliefs really do not drive a church's culture. Any new behaviors need to be consistent with the beliefs. But beliefs are usually not the place to start the cultural change process. Work first on behaviors that express the beliefs.

All churches say they value mission to others. They recognize and accept the Great Commission to take the Gospel to others. But somehow many never get around to doing much about it. Their own immediate congregational needs take priority, especially if they are financially challenged. How dollars are spent is a fairly good measure of value placed. Another good measure is time spent. Does any body go out of the way to serve someone else beyond the congregation? Probably some do so individually on their own. But is this a shared church value?

The way to find out is for a leader to propose some specific mission-minded behaviors that do not cost anything but time. The minister could preach ten sermons on the Great Commission, but the values of a church's culture will not change until some new behaviors emerge. This will happen best if doable, specific opportunities are organized and made accessible. To change a church culture, start with specific behaviors, then deal with the differing values.

Basic Underlying Assumptions

Organizational culture specialist Edgar Schein makes a helpful distinction between espoused beliefs and values and then the barely expressed basic assumptions underlying an organizational culture. Most difficulties in remodeling a culture come not from dealing with stated beliefs but from running into unstated underlying assumptions. These basic assumptions are difficult to confront, tend to be non-debatable and hence are extremely difficult to change. Such assumptions are called "theories in use" in the field. Congregations often have theories-in-use that have little relation to the espoused theology.

Thousands are the stories of pastors who come to a congregation with the intent to take it in a new direction only to discover stiff, debilitating resistance in a year or so, to the dissatisfaction of all. The desired change is usually in the direction of turning around decline by worship and program changes intended to be more appealing to the unchurched. Often the pastor has the assurance of the call committee that the new direction is exactly what they want. The basic underlying, unexpressed assumption for most members, however, is that their church culture should stay the way it is. Of course they want the pastor to bring new members, but usually taken for granted is that the new ones should be like the present ones, enjoying and doing what they themselves enjoy and do.

Behaviors

The positive behaviors to aim for in changing a church's culture have been discussed in previous chapters and in the previous section of this chapter. Congregations are encouraged to:

Ask the Father to send the Spirit in specific ways. In appropriate circumstances, tell stories of how the Spirit worked recently. Celebrate progress in personal spiritual journeys, especially in the form of major awakenings to a higher level of spiritual understanding. Offer a greater variety of opportunities for spiritual experiences. Be willing to recognize God's supernatural interventions in healings and to pray for them.

Influences on Behavior in Congregations

What are the options church leaders have for ways to change behaviors in a congregation and thus its culture? Right out of my M.B.A. class lectures for the Social Psychology of Work Organizations, I offer four sources of influence on the behavior of those doing cooperative effort:

1. Formal messages are mostly expectations put into writing, such as job descriptions, goal and policy statements, messages of encouragement.

In churches, look for policy statements, by-laws, and of course sermons. Unlike other organizations, churches have a pulpit with expectations for a formal message each week. Any anticipated change needs to have the reasons for it enunciated. Basic to good communication is to use mostly words familiar to the listener and therefore to speak and write with lots of words from the church's tradition, adding just a few new words or concepts gradually. Remember, culture trumps vision.

2. Informal group messages that affect behavior are those of others in the work group who interpret what they should really pay attention to and thus what can be ignored. The filter is usually whether or not there will be any consequences for ignoring what the boss says.

Church people usually bring powerful filters with them, especially if they have heard hundreds of sermons. For those who come to church out of habit, the first challenge is to get and hold attention. The filter is whether the message applies to them personally. The preachers in my church are working on ending each sermon with next steps and then having these listed for check off on a Connection Card gathered after the message. The next steps usually involve some specific activities.

Two different kinds of church cultures can be distinguished on the basis of the informal conversation of participants after the service is over. In my tradition this is mostly small talk that could be heard in almost any social setting. I admire those churches where participants actually talk about the message or service and bring God into their conversations. Getting from the first to the second is a tall challenge.

3. **Technique messages** are delivered by the established work flow. Keeping up with the assembly line determines most of the behavior of factory workers. Office workers find themselves spending hours in front of a computer screen. As is so evident in recent decades, new technologies necessitate different behaviors.

"Technique" is a good word for church use. A worship service employs many different techniques, such as how prayer is done. Is it exclusively by the pastor reading written prayers or delivered informally? Does the congregation join together speaking written prayers or are they encouraged to break into small groups for shared prayer about what is on their minds? Is the order of service taken from a hymnal, or from a folder customized for that weekend, or presented on an overhead screen? Is the singing done sitting down or standing up, led by an organ or a praise band, from the front or the back? These are just illustrations to raise awareness. A good exercise would be to note all the different techniques used in a worship service and then think back on alternatives that could be tried instead.

Church cultures are traditions developed as customs, and customs are made up of accepted techniques. The easiest way to start changing a culture is to try specific new techniques. The easiest techniques to change are those usually regarded as the pastor's prerogative, such as standing behind a pulpit or by the first pew, or leading prayers differently. But at some point, small changes add up to new customs that raise anxiety about whether the old ways were inadequate, and members feel devalued. Then the leader is dealing with basic assumptions that are barely recognized. That is when the skills for managing church conflict are put to the test.

4. Action messages are what participants find themselves actually doing. Words have turned into action. If they find themselves cleaning someone else's house on a Saturday morning, they are asking basic questions and rediscovering values that their church stands for. Usually such activity needs to be organized to provide an occasion.

In general, the influence of a message source on behavior goes from the most powerful at the bottom to the least powerful at the top of this list. Action messages are the most influential, while formal messages are the least. Most church cultures assume the top down approach and too often never get to action messages. If you want to change a church culture, change what participants actually do; move beyond just preaching about it.

Of the sixteen action steps listed earlier in this chapter, focus on the one or two that can accomplished most easily and successfully. Move on from there.

How Nehemiah Changed an Old Testament Culture

The Old Testament Book of Nehemiah offers a great illustration of how to change a church culture. The year was about 448 B.C. Nehemiah, from the community of Jewish exiles in Babylon, was a court administrator for King Artaxerxes. He felt called to take a leave of absence to return home to help his kinsmen rebuild the Jerusalem walls that were destroyed in

587 B.C., when Judah rebelled against Babylon.

On site after assessing the situation for three days, Nehemiah called together the Jerusalem leaders, focusing attention on the obvious security problem of having no walls. Then he announced his plan. The next day all Jewish men found themselves hauling stones and beams and witnessing progress restoring the wall. For most, action came before understanding the full rationale.

It was crucial that Nehemiah organized assignments according to family or neighborhood groupings—so important that the names and assignments are all preserved in Chapter 3. There was lots of social pressure to conform to the plan. Nehemiah knew how to work through natural group leaders and let them fill in the specifics in their own way.

After the wall was built in only 52 days, Ezra, their spiritual leader, gathered everybody before the Water Gate and read the Law, the Word of God, all morning, and the Levites then explained it. On the 28th day Ezra led them all in a time of repentance followed by a covenant agreement which the leaders signed. Then the wall was dedicated. Ezra and Nehemiah made one of the greatest preacher/administrator teams of all times.

The sequence was action messages of specific behaviors, supported by group messages and finalized with dramatic formal messages.

Hope for a Remnant

Many Christian churches in America today face the kind of future the Israelites experienced before the return of Ezra and Nehemiah. Those chosen people of God were a discouraged remnant of what used to be a flourishing and exciting community. Today the effects of the accelerating 50-year decline of traditional Protestant church bodies are making evident that a very large proportion of congregations are well along in the withering process—mostly gray hair with few young families and shrinking numbers as the elderly pass on.

That Israelite remnant must have thought God had abandoned them. Of course, he had not. God had many plans for his people. But his ways took new forms when he sent his Son to call forth a new people of God that became Christianity. Then he called the Apostle Paul to new experiences of the timeless Holy Spirit and to explain to Christ's follower how the Spirit works in their lives.

Withering Christian congregations need to ask what kind of problem they are facing. Do they have a God problem that he has abandoned them? Or is the problem that their particular traditional church culture no longer fits well with the emerging changes in American culture.

The fact is that God's Christian church is alive and flourishing in other parts of the world. The Holy Spirit is changing an ever increasing number of people around the world. Just as the Israelites at Nehemiah's time could not anticipate what God did in the New Testament 450 years later, so American Protestants just 100 years ago could not have anticipated the rise of highly Spirit-oriented Christians here and around the world.

Here is the choice: Protestant congregations can insist on staying with all of the traditions and forms they know from previous generations. Or they can watch how the Spirit is moving today and open themselves step by step to such movement in their midst. Is a congregation's cultural heritage definitive for all times, or can it be a solid foundation for remodeling that stays better in step with the Spirit and times?

A good leader will help the congregation make an informed choice about how they will face the future. Some fresh movement of the Holy Spirit will have to happen in order to step up to such choice, let alone make it.

Accept the challenge to cultivate the soil of church life and to open up the vents for the Spirit's pneumatic power. Take the challenge of sailing close to the Spirit wind. Ask the Father to send his Holy Spirit to guide the process. Then see what happens. You might be surprised!

The wind blows wherever it pleases. You hear its sound, but youcannot tell where it comes from or where it is going. So it is with everyone shaped by the Spirit.
John 3:8

Discussion Guide for

Introduction
What Has the Holy Spirit Done in Your Life Lately?

1. What is your response to this question:

"What has the Holy Spirit done in your life lately? The Spirit brought you into saving faith. True. But what about lately, say, in the last month or two?"

2. How well does the following statement describe your view?

"Too often we gain the impression that the Spirit was some kind of vague ghostly presence only in Bible times."

3. What is your reaction to the rhythm of Name an encounter with the Spirit, Share it with others, and Seek More?

4. How can Jesus' famous promise of a response to asking, seeking, and knocking make more sense when applied to asking for the Holy Spirit?

"My answer is that he wants us to ask for specific movements of the Spirit among specific people. He wants us to form clear expectations so that we can observe when in fact the Spirit has moved. We are more likely to see what we expect than to notice something we are not looking for." "Christians can be trained to see what many other Christians miss."

5. What is supernatural motivation?

"Appealing to the more basic human needs (bodily, security, affiliation, status) did indeed enable the Spirit to energize Christian churches over the centuries. But human motivation alone has its limits, especially as our American culture becomes increasingly unchurched. It is time to learn how to appeal to the supernatural motivation offered by the Holy Spirit." "In terms of human motivation this can be called 'self actualization.'"

6. What is the difference between emotions and reason in church life?

"Here is the issue: Do the emotions come first before you rationally figure them out? Such "raw" emotions are too often not of the Spirit and can become destructive. Or do feelings flow from reasonable perceptions based on Scriptures? Such feelings can be the bedrock of church life."

The Holy Spirit shapes human spirit.
John 3: 6
Discussion Guide to

CHAPTER 1
How Do People Experience God in Their Lives?

1. Is there a more basic question for Christians and their leaders to ask in this 21st century than, How do people experience God in their lives today?

"Ways that previous generations experienced God are not working as well now in younger generations. When and how do believers attach trust and feelings to the Gospel? Faith without feelings remains superficial and probably boring."

2. Can you tell when a person's "spirit" has changed for the worse? for the better? How? Can you envision how the Holy Spirit has anything to do with this?

3. Have you personally experienced any of the following?
- Greater understanding of faith?
- Less temptation?
- Less enslavement to fears?
- Desire to do more ministry in church?
- More willingness to sacrifice something?
- A special feel of unity with other Christians?
- A greater sense of love, joy, peace, patience, gentleness?

4. Have you witnessed the Spirit at work in others?

- Someone encountering Christ's call and deciding to follow?
- Presentations of the Word that bring greater insight?
- Someone's new life in Christ becoming more evident?
- Someone coming to church through a personal invitation?
- Better relationships when two or three come together in Christ?
- A Christian showing special boldness or wisdom in witnessing?
- Christians singing with special gusto and intensity.
- Someone experiencing freshness and renewal in their faith?

5. Can you envision the Holy Spirit as a dove sitting on your shoulder and whispering into your ear something God would have you do?

Can you recall a time when you heard such a whisper of the Spirit and acted on it?

6. How can you tell when it is the Spirit whispering?
What do you think of Jonathan Edwards' distinction between unreliable and reliable signs of the Spirit?

    Reliable Signs:
- a lasting indwelling that brings an evident new nature,
- a new spiritual sense that does not come from self-interest,
- new kind of conviction and humility,
- hunger for God,
- Christian practice.

*Now about spiritual gifts, brothers,
I do not want you to be ignorant.*
(1 Corinthians 12:1)

Discussion Guide to

CHAPTER 2
Seek the Gifts and Fruit of the Spirit

1. What, if any, has been your experience with Paul's teaching on spiritual gifts in 1 Corinthians 12?

2. Have you witnessed special energy for ministry?

"Paul's major point in 1 Corinthians 12 is that in each congregation of believers the Spirit is already at work motivating all participants to contribute different acts of ministry for the common good. This is motivation very different from reluctantly serving on a committee."

3. What has been your experience with Paul's teaching on fruit of the Spirit?

"He distinguishes a subset of spiritual gifts that he calls the greater gifts for the most excellent way of living together as a congregation. Chief is love, without which fulfilling life together is difficult. To the Galatians he describes these as fruit of the Spirit."

4. What are the fruit of the Spirit?

Which words would you use to describe what the fruit of the Spirit are that Paul lists in Galatians 5: 22: love, joy, peace, patience, kindness, goodness, faithfulness, gentleness and self-control?

Are they: Emotions? Feelings? Characteristics? Something else?

5. How are the fruit of the Spirit related to fellowship?

In his benediction at the end of his first letter to the Corinthians, Paul chooses "fellowship" as the key characteristic of the Holy Spirit. "May the grace of the Lord Jesus Christ and the love of God and the *fellowship* of the Holy Spirit be with you all."

6. What do you know about Pentecostal churches and the charismatic movement of the 1960s and 70s?

"By any standard, the growth of Pentecostal expressions of Christianity has been phenomenal. A hundred years after its start in 1906, the movement worldwide was estimated to include 558,000,000 adherents."

Do not conform any longer to the pattern of the present time.
Romans 12:2

Discussion Guide to
CHAPTER 3
The Spirit Brings Growth Beyond Conformity

1. Do you or anyone in your group have experience with life in a village or small town? What is your impression of the emphasis on conformity in village life?

2. When the proportion of a population goes from 90% rural and small town to 90% urban, what can you expect to occur in the traditions of a congregation in the new setting? Said differently, what can you expect to no longer happen in urban church life as it used to in villages?

3. How important do you think freshness and change are in a church?

"In contrast to such conformity, the Apostle Paul recognized that the hallmark of the Holy Spirit at work is freshness and change."

4. Do you agree?

"Many congregations and pastors wind up doing the same old things with the same people in the same old ways and thereby close the door on what new things the Spirit might want to do among them. The Spirit's inclination is to change people, not leave them in a rut."

5. Can you recognize these as remnants of village-style ministry?

   a. 14-year-old confirmation of children baptized as infants

   b. Emphasis on separation between clergy and laity.

   Are there any other remnants of village church culture you can recognize today?

6. What is the definition of Christian maturity in a village church?

   Compare that to Paul's definition:

   "Paul's understanding of maturity is quite different. No one ever reaches it. He tells the Ephesians that their local body of Christ should continue to be built up until all become mature, reaching to the height of Christ's full stature (Ephesians 4:13). Because the standard is Christ-likeness, we will never reach full maturity as a Christian in this life."

7. What is your reaction to the claim that for Paul life in Christ and life in the Spirit are one and the same thing.

   "They are two ways of describing the same experience. To become more Christ like is to be filled more by the Holy Spirit."

Others, like seed sown on good soil, hear the word, accept it and produce a crop. Mark 4:20

Discussion Guide to

CHAPTER 4
Cultivate the Soil of Personal and Church Life

1. What is your first reaction to using the metaphor of cultivating the soil of personal and church life to prepare for the Spirit's fresh movement?

2. How useful for you are these three images for approaching God in repentance.

   a. The Pharisee and Publican (Luke 18)

   b. God resists the proud but gives grace to the humble. (James 4:6)

   c. Isaiah's "Woe is me. I am ruined." (Isaiah 6:5)

3. What would you look for to see a hard path, rocks or weeds in your personal spiritual life? (page 51)

4. What would happen if a pastor would view the congregation as the topsoil for pastoral work?

5. Does your congregation have hard soil and how would you break them up?

6. Does the soil of your congregation have a lot of rocks, and how would you deal with them?

7. Does your congregation have weeds in its soil? What would you look for? How would you deal with them?

8. Can you imagine calling your whole congregation to a day of repentance? What should it repent of? How would you envision that happening on such a Sunday?

Since we live by the Spirit, let us keep in step with the Spirit.
Galatians 5:25

Discussion Guide to

CHAPTER 5
Share More Stories of Personal Spiritual Journeys

1. Can you recall a car of yours whose odometer (count of miles traveled) brings back happy memories? Why?

2. Share a little bit of your personal spiritual journey in Christ. When did it star? What were high points? Would you care to share any low points?

3. Luke uses the unique and helpful phrase "full of the Holy Spirit," which he then couples with a specific characteristic to describe what that fullness brought: joy, wisdom, faith, witnessing boldly.

Can you recall a time when you were unusually "full of the Spirit"?

4. React to this interpretation of Paul.

He wanted primarily that believers be filled by the Holy Spirit to the point of having so much of the Spirit that his gifts and fruit overflow in their lives of abundance.

5. Another description envisions a productive Christian "hitting the wall."—an obstacle they cannot overcome with their ordinary efforts and skills. Have you ever "hit the wall" or do you know someone who has?

6. How important is struggle in a Christian's spiritual journey?

"Struggle cannot be taught. It happens one by one through personal response to unique circumstances. But we can observe what it is like in others and learn how God worked it out their lives. It is the personal struggle of a "before" condition that sets up the compelling "after" story of a movement to greater convictional faith.

7. Do you or your church have a good balance between Spirit and Memory?

When a church lives just on Memories it loses touch with God. An excess of Spirit, however, needs to be corrected with Memory of what has happened in such circumstances in the past.

8. What is your reaction to focusing on awakenings rather than on conversions?

The wind blows wherever it pleases. You hear its sound, but you cannot tell where it comes from or where it is going. So it is with everyone born of the Spirit.
John 3:8

Discussion Guide to

CHAPTER 6
Modify Your Church Culture to Thrive Spiritually

1. Is "passionate spirituality" characteristic of your congregation?

"In discussions I have had with leaders in traditional church bodies, someone will inevitably observe that "passionate" and their tradition are an oxymoron—a contradiction. This is a sure formula for decline."

2. How can a congregation purposely decide to thrive spiritually?

3. What meanings have you heard applied to the word "spirituality"?

"If you are talking spirituality but are not focused on the Holy Spirit, then you are not talking biblical Christian spirituality."

4. Which is the greater danger for your church?

Two kinds of fears can drive their decision making in a church. One is having so much spiritual energy that the fellowship bursts apart from all the activity. The other is having so little spiritual energy that their church fades away.

5. Do you have experience with a short-term mission trip or a weekend renewal event? How can they become a spiritual experience?

6. Have you experienced or do you know someone who experienced a miracle, defined as an unusual event for which there is no natural explanation?

7. Does your church heritage teach that miracles ceased after the New Testament? What is your reaction?

8. Have you ever struggled with modern university culture that assumes a one-dimensional view of the world—all that exists is what can be observed and measured?

Come, let us rebuild the wall of Jerusalem and we will no longer be in disgrace. I also told them about the gracious hand of my God upon me and what the king had said to me. They replied, "Let us start rebuilding."

Nehemiah 2: 18

Discussion Guide to

CHAPTER 7

Change the Behavior To Change the Culture

1. American institutions are undergoing rapid change because they now face more competition and higher expectations. Do you think this is true for churches, too?

2. Corporate cultures have been purposely and steadily changing in recent decades. Have you experienced culture change at work or in schools?

3. What do you recognize in the culture of your congregation that could be changed without changing basic beliefs?

4. Why is changing an organization's culture anxiety provoking?

5. How does "culture trumps vision"?.

'Vision is about *ideas*. Culture is *behavior*. Culture change is all about turning new ideas into new action that past behaviors would resist."

6. What are some of the unstated assumptions that that would make culture change difficult in your church?

"A helpful distinction is between espoused beliefs and values and then the barely expressed basic assumptions underlying an organizational culture."

7. How helpful is the distinction between formal messages, like sermons and job description, and the action message that participants find themselves doing?

8. What are the most helpful things you have learned in these discussions of Alive in the Spirit?

Key Passages on the Work of the Holy Spirit Today

The Holy Spirit shapes human spirit.
John 3: 6

*The wind blows wherever it pleases. You hear its sound,
but you cannot tell where it comes from or where it is going.
So it is with everyone born of the Spirit.*
John 3:8

*I will ask the Father, and he will give you another advocate to be with you
forever—the Spirit of truth. You know him, for he lives with you and will be
in you. I will not leave you as orphans.*
John 14: 15-16

*But the Counselor, the Holy Spirit, whom the Father will send in my name,
will teach you all things and will remind you of everything I have said to you.*
John 14 26

*If fathers know how to give good gifts to their children, how much
more will your heavenly Father give the Holy Spirit to those who
ask him!*
Luke 11: 13

*Those who live according to the sinful nature have their minds
set on what that nature desires; but those who live in accordance
with the Spirit have their mind set on what the Spirit desires.*
Romans 8: 5

*If the Spirit of him who raised Jesus from the dead is living in
you, he who raised Christ from the dead will also give life to your
mortal bodies through his Spirit, who lives in you.*
Romans 8: 11

Rev. David S. Luecke, Ph.D.

Now about spiritual gifts, brothers, I do not want you to be ignorant.
1 Corinthians 12:1

Now to each one the manifestation of the Spirit is given for the common good.
1 Corinthians 12:7

You show that you are a letter from Christ, the result of our ministry, written not with ink but with the Spirit of the living God, not on tablets of stone but on tablets of human hearts.
2 Corinthians: 3: 3

The Lord is the Spirit, and where the Spirit of the Lord is, there is freedom.
2 Corinthians 3: 17

And we who reflect the Lord's glory are being transformed into his like-ness with ever-increasing glory, which comes from the Lord, who is the Spirit.
2 Corinthians 3: 18

The grace of our Lord Jesus Christ, the love of God the Father and the fellowship of the Holy Spirit be with you all.
2 Corinthians 13:14

The fruit of the Spirit is love, joy, peace, patience, kindness, goodness, faithfulness, gentleness and self-control
Galatians 5: 22

Since we live by the Spirit, let us keep in step with the Spirit.
Galatians 5:25

End Notes

[1] J. Harold Ellens, Understanding Religious Experiences: What the Bible Says about Spirituality, Praeger, 2008, p. 98.

[2] Gordon F. Fee, God's Empowering Presence, Hendrickson Publishers, 1994. p. 825

[3] T. M. Luhrmann, When God Talks Back: Understanding the American Evangelical Relationship with God, Knopf, 2012, xix, xxi

[4] Robert D. Putnam, Bowling Alone: The Collapse and Revival of American Community, Simon and Scuster, 2000.

[5] Diana Butler Bass, Christianity After Religion: The End of Church and the Birth of a New Spiritual Awakening, Harper One, 2012, p. 120.

[6] Matthew A. Elliott, Faithful Feelings: Rethinking Emotion in the New Testament, Kregel, 2006, pp. 18-52.

[7] Gerald R. McDermott, Seeing God: Twelve Reliable Signs of True Spirituality, Intervarsity Press, 1995, p. 31,32.

[8] Ralph W. Hood, "The Facilitation of Religious Experience," in Handbook of Religious Experience, ed. Ralph W. Hood, Religious Education Press, 1995, p. 577.

[9] H. Newton Malony, Psychology of Religions: Personalities, Problems, Possibilities, ed by H. Newton Malony, Baker, 1991, p. 203. Another helpful text is Psychology and Religion: Classic and Contemporary Views, by Davd M. Wulff, John Wiley, 1991.

[10] J. T. Richardson, "The active vs passive convert: Paradigm conflict in conversion/recruitment research." Journal for the Scientific Study of Religion. 1985, pp. 166-172., as found in Ralph W. Hood, Bernard Spilka, Bruce Humsberger, Richard Gorsuch, The Psychology of Religion: An Empirical Approach, 2nd Edition, Guildor Press,1996, p.283.

[11] J. Harold Ellens, Understanding Religious Experiences, Praeger, 2008, p. 94.

[12] David S. Luecke, Talking With God: How Ordinary Christians Grow in Prayer, Fellowship Ministries, 1997, p. 59, 60.

[13]"Changes in American Megachurches: Tracing Eight Years of Growth and Innovation in the Nation's Largest-attendance Congregations," Scott Thumma and Warren Bird, Hartford Institute for Religion Research, 2008

[14]The Book of Concord, Smalcald Articles, Part III, Article IV.

[15]Karl Rahner, The Spirit in the Church, 1977.

[16]Brian Kolodiejchuk, Mother Teresa: Come By My Light: The Private Writings of the Saint of Calcutta, Crown Publishing, 2007.

[17]Bill Hybels, The Power of a Whisper, Hearing God and Having the Guts to Respond, 2010, p 43-44.

[18]Dallas Willard, Hearing God: Developing a Conversational Relationship with God, Inter Varsity Press, 1999, p. 170.

[19]Gerald R. McDermott, Seeing God: Twelve Reliable Signs of True Spirituality, Intervarsity Press, 1995, p. 32-41.

[20]Grant McClug, "Pentecostals: the Sequel," Christianity Today, April 1, 2006

[21]Donald E. Miller and Tetsunao Yamamori, Global Pentecostalism: The New Face of Christian Social Engagement, University of California Press, 2007, pp.26-28.

[22]Charles J. Keating, Who We Are Is How We Pray, Twenty-Third Publications, 1987.

[23]Gary Thomas, Sacred Pathways: Discover Your Soul's Path to God, Zondervan, 2000, pp 215.

[24]"Changes in American Megachurches: Tracing Eight Years of Growth and Innovation in the Nation's Largest-attendance Congregations," Scott Thumma and Warren Bird, Hartford Institute for Religion Research, 2008

[25]Jonathan Edwards, "Personal Narrative," in Jonathan Edwards: Basic Writings, ed. Ola Winslow, Penguin, 1966, p.85.

[26]Eugene H. Peterson, Under the Unpedictable Plant, Eerdmans, 1992, p. 134.

[27]Robert Fuller, Spiritual but Not Religious: Understanding Unchurched America, Oxford, 2001, p.6 as quoted in Diane Butler Bass, Christianity

after Religion, HarperOne, 2012, p. 67.

[28]Diane Butler Bass, Christianity after Religion: The End of Church and the Birth of a New Spiritual Awakening, Harper One, 2012.

Andrew Farley, God without Religion: Can it Really Be This Simple? Baker Books, 2011.

Rick James, Jesus without Religion, IVP Books, 2007.

[29]Ellens, p. 96.

[30]James W. Jones, The Spirit and the World, Hawthorn, 1975, pp 33, 41, 44.

[31]C. F. W. Walther, "We are No Longer What We Were," in Selected Sermons of C.F.W. Walther, tr. Henry Eggold, Concordia Publishing House, 1981, pp. 155-163.

[32]Greg L. Hawkins, Cally Parkinson and Eric Arneson, Reveal, Willow Creek Resources, 2007.

[33]Janet O. Hagbert and Robert A. Guelich, The Critical Journey: Stages in the Life of Faith, Word Publishing, 1989, p. 10.

[34]James W. Fowler. Stages of Faith: The Psychology of Human Development and the Quest for Meaning, Harper One, 1995.

[35]James E. Loder, The Transforming Moment, second ed., Helmers and Howard, 1989, p. 10.

[36]Gordon D. Fee, "On Getting the Spirit Back into Spirituality," in Life in the Spirit, ed. Jeffrey Greenman and George Kalantzis, IVP, 2010, p. 43.

[37]John Shea, An Experience Named Spirit, Thomas More Press, 1983.

[38]Leonard Sweet, Post Modern Pilgrims, 2000, Broadman and Holman.

[39]Ralph W. Hook, Bernard Spilka, Bruce Humsberger, Richard Gorsuch, The Psychology of Religion: An Empirical Approach, 2nd Edition, Guildor Press, 1996, p.283.

[40]Greg L Hawkins, Cally Parkinson, Move: What 1,000 Churches REVEAL about Spiritual Growth, Zondervan, 2011.

[41] Christian A. Schwarz, Natural Church Development: A Guide to Eight Essential Qualities of Healthy Churches, Church Smart, 1998, pp 22-37.

[42] Max Lucado, Come Thirsty, W Publishing Group, 2004, p. 60.

[43] Loren E. Halverson, "Prayer and Action," in A Primer on Prayer, ed. by Paul R. Sponheim, Fortress, 1988, p. 98.

[44] Rebecca Button Prichard, 'Do Miracles Still Happen?' Presbyterians Today, March 1999.

[45] Bengt Hoffman, Luther and the Mystics, Augsburg, 1976, pp. 195-200.

[46] Ken Blue, Authority to Heal, IVP, 1987.

[47] Rober Wuthnow, After Heaven: Spirituality in America Since the 1950s, University of California Press, 1998, p. 122.

[48] Craig S. Keener, Miracles: The Credibility of the New Testament Accounts, Baker Academic, p. 201, 203.

[49] Paul Prather, Modern-Day Miracles: How Ordinary People Experience Supernatural Acts of God, Andres and McMeel, 1996, p. 66.

[50] Christian A. Schwarz, Natural Church Development: A Guide to Eight Essential Qualities of Healthy Churches, Church Smart Resources, 3rd edition, 1998.

[51] Edgar H. Schein, Organizational Culture and Leadership, fourth edition, Jossey Bass, 2010,

www.ingramcontent.com/pod-product-compliance
Ingram Content Group UK Ltd.
Pitfield, Milton Keynes, MK11 3LW, UK
UKHW020244240426
12048UKWH00026B/1595